Praise for **THE DELIBERATE EFFEC**

"Tarina's willingness to delve into her own experiences and deeply reflect on them is a benefit for the scores of people who want to make the world a better place but aren't sure how do it. The Deliberate Effect is not only an incredibly easy read that keeps you glued to the pages but it also keeps you wishing it would never end!"

– **Bob Proctor, world-renowned speaker and coach,** *New York Times* **bestselling author and star of the movie** *The Secret*

"This book is easy to read and powerful in its message and teaching. The content is inspiring; Tarina logically and playfully describes how our choices and actions affect every aspect of our lives and how to use them in our greatest favor. I can tell you from my own experiences that your success really is most definitely determined by what and how you think. The Deliberate Effect captures that message and more!"

– **Peggy McColl,**
New York Times **Bestselling Author**

"The Deliberate Effect is heartfelt, compelling, and inspirational. Each chapter relates an important lesson in life that Tarina learned from actual experiences she has gone through. This book is both a terrific story and a guide to making a difference in the world. I highly recommend."

– **Emmanuel Dagher, Two-Time Bestselling Author of** *Easy Breezy Prosperity* **and** *Easy Breezy Miracle*

"Inspiring, thought provoking, and deeply meaningful, **The Deliberate Effect** *profoundly resonated with me and it will resonate with you. Reading this book has made me think outside the box. A book worth reading for everyone, but especially those who are still figuring out what their personal calling is."*

– **Judy O'Beirn, International Bestselling Author of** **the** *Unwavering Strength* **series**

*"Not only does this book provide a detailed how-to perspective on how you start something or change something but also offers insight into the often ignored emotional, physical, and psychological ups and downs of this process. After reading **The Deliberate Effect**, not only do I feel like I CAN do anything, I also feel like I WANT to go do EVERYTHING! Great Read!"*

– Dr. Joe Rubino,
www.CenterForPersonalReinvention.com

*"**The Deliberate Effect** is inspirational and insightful and I have never identified more with a book. This book really makes you feel like you can achieve amazing things if you set your mind to it while taking small steps. A must-read if you've ever had a chorus of "I can't" singing in your head!"*

– Wendy Ditta,
Bestselling Author of *The More I Learn, The More I Love*

*"Tarina W's inspiring and enchanting new book explains that while most of us intuitively know that the attitudes and mindset we adopt will influence how our day and our lives unfold, but we don't ever think about changing it to get different results. If we approach our days with optimism, then our days will unfold in a positive way; if we approach our days with pessimism, our days unfold negatively. **The Deliberate Effect** is full of tools you can start applying to your life right away so that you can deliberately choose to live your life the way you want to!"*

– George Jerjian,
Consultant, Speaker and Author of *Spirit of Gratitude*

*"In **The Deliberate Effect**, Tarina offers several methods and principles for maintaining a positive mental attitude and for avoiding a negative mental attitude. You'll find lots of great tips to help you focus on your goals and take command of your life. Don't hold back – make your dreams happen!"*

– Susan Shumsky,
Author of *Miracle Prayer* and 13 other books

"Go get this book! Read it, absorb it, and be inspired! Through Tarina W's unique and deeply personal (and often hilarious!) approach, **The Deliberate Effect** will be your quintessential guide to BECOME your best self. Tarina W's masterful insights, as told through her 20+ years of experiences and research, stories and philosophies, resonate long after being immersed in her stories and masterfully relate to personal and work lives. 'Choose. Act. Become.' It's deliberate message will become your new mantra."

– **Terri Harrison,**
Life Enthusiast and Vice President at
TAP Strategy & HR Consulting

"With humour, humility and a hands on approach, Tarina has harnessed the ability to empower individuals, parents, leaders and entrepreneurs with deliberate vision and skills to rise above the distractions that prevent you from reaching self actualisation and living your life the way YOU want to!"

– **Vanessa Robillard,**
Chairperson and Program Coordinator of the
Social Service Program at Dawson College

"Tarina is defined by three key words: Insight, Perspective and Action. Her coaching style and way of life are to make moments matter and to drive to results you've deliberately planned out. She's able to inspire, motivate and teach in a special way. Her new book embodies all of this and brings the reader close to the power that deliberate living can bring! A great read!"

– **Rob Clendenning,**
Technology Management Consultant

"Tarina is my go-to expert when it comes to leading and living a purposeful life. Just like she did for me, she will guide you on a rewarding journey of cutting out the noise in your life and helping you gain time and energy to focus on what's truly important to you."

– **Caroline Barth,**
Head of Global HR, Novartis Pharmaceuticals

"Tarina's depth of knowledge, experience and her special abilities has allowed me to take my ideals and express them through improved leadership skills into my organization. Her insights on leadership, perception and techniques are very powerful. She is an inspirational teacher, coach and mentor all in one package!"

– **Livio Di Francesco,**
General Manager of Paladin Labs

STOP DOING IT ALL. START DOING WHAT MATTERS.

THE *Deliberate* EFFECT

CHOOSE

ACT

BECOME

TARINA W.

Published by
Hasmark Publishing
www.hasmarkpublishing.com

Permission should be addressed in writing to Tarina Wagschal at info@tarinaw.com or 51 Cartier Ave., Pointe-Claire QC H9S 4R5

Editor & Illustrator: Anna Rosenfield

Cover Designer & Layout Artist: Anne Karklins

ISBN 13: 978-1-989161-28-9
ISBN 10: 1989161286

To my Family of Five who put up with me,
allow me to lead them,
and whose love for me is raw and complete.

Mom, Robert, Nicholas, Tristan, and Emma-Girl:
this is all for you and because of you.

May you always think of me as you make your own choices,
live and love in action, and become what matters to YOU most.
If you do that and only that (and come to the cottage often!),
know my heart is abundantly happy and satisfied,
Forever and a Day.

CONTENTS

BECOME WHAT MATTERS

Sustaining, Protecting, and Ever-Evolving Your Deliberate Life

FOREWORD

In today's fast-paced, highly competitive world, more than ever people are on the hunt for effective tools that can help them manage, overcome and adapt to life's demands. Fortunately, the solution to creating and sustaining a fulfilling life amidst the challenges can be found in Tarina W.'s life-changing new book, *The Deliberate Effect*. If you are beginning to explore the field of personal development, this book is sure to give you more joy, positive thinking and an affinity to action with ease.

When Tarina asked me to write the Foreword for this book I was delighted and honored. Her message is relatable and authentic, with her real-life stories complementing inspiring and tangible ways to help you live your best life. This book is a guide that is easy to get drawn into and packed with simple tools that you can immediately begin to leverage for your growth.

As time passes and knowledge accumulates, what you once learned may no longer work and making changes can be a challenge. Tarina has an uncanny insight into one's ingrained habits and shares inspirational ways to identify and then transform these habits. With powerful truths tucked into each chapter, Tarina helps to free readers from their own self-imposed limiting self-concepts so that they can begin their journey toward living a remarkable life.

Tarina simplifies concepts that can otherwise intimidate: dismantling negative patterns, gaining clarity on your priorities, and setting up the goals to achieve whatever you want in your life are some of the many she uncovers. The exercises provided in addition to her insights are simple yet powerful – my feeling is that you will be amazed at what you come to find in your own life from engaging with them, and I encourage you to do so.

> *"Plant the seed of what you want in your mind*
> *to get what you want out of life."*
> – Mike Tate

This is not your typical book about "thinking positively", it's far more comprehensive and concrete, offering guidance to change those interior feelings, and then translating them to your outer experiences.

Through expansive and highly accessible processes, *The Deliberate Effect* serves as a handbook that provides an empowering roadmap to discovering personal fulfillment and freedom. Its succinct, easy-to-read teachings will enable you to experience a remarkable life that matters to you.

This book helps you turn what you're reading into ACTION.

It's about taking charge of your life, NOW.

If you are looking to triumph in all areas, turn the page and dive right in.

This book is a wonderful addition to the personal development world of reading and the perfect place to start your journey.

Peggy McColl,
New York Times Best Selling Author

AUTHOR'S NOTE

Before December 2013, everyone seemed to feel I had it all. So did I.

Then suddenly, I didn't.

It's amazing how, no matter how hard we try to forget it, we can never truly anticipate what's ahead of us. I know that when I was on that beach in Turks and Caicos with my love of 18 years and our three teens safely tucked away at home with my mom, life seemed as though it just couldn't get any better. Returning to Montreal after those two relaxing weeks with my husband, Robert, I felt light, at peace, and so grateful – for my beautiful life, the health of our family, and for being so blessed as to enjoy such a luxurious vacation.

Within a few moments of walking in the door, I knew something was wrong. Usually my mom would stay up and greet us, but she had already gone home and left a note saying she had a headache. That was five years ago and her headaches still persist. It turns out that while babysitting our kids she suffered a concussion, which evolved into a rare form of post-concussion syndrome. In an instant, my free-spirited, book-loving, young and hip mom was forever changed.

Little did I know, that was only the beginning of the landslide.

Up to that point in our lives, big incidents didn't happen in our family. Robert and I are two successful professionals and dedicated parents with a close-knit, loving family. Really bad things didn't happen to us – we planned it so. Then, as life sometimes goes, our plans drifted out the window and a storm blew in.

Fast-forward to a mere week after our arrival home and my kids are videotaping their nurturing, loving, secure dad sprawled across our bed utterly incomprehensible. They were petrified and so was I; we had never seen this before. *Did he have a brain injury? Was this a sudden onset of Alzheimer's?* No, we realized. Instead, my husband – their father – was totally drunk and had reached a frightening crescendo of intoxication before our eyes. Were there signs? In retrospect, of course, there were signs. But it's always different in hindsight. Perhaps I failed to realize it sooner because it scared me too much to address. The next morning we showed him the video and, with tears streaming down his face, he announced that right after Christmas he would leave his law practice to check himself into rehab for a month. He wanted to be the father and husband he'd always been and take a proactive approach to the situation. He knew he could either try and do this on his own or get laser-focused and deal with his problem before it took over.

On January 13, 2014, I dropped Robert off at a rehab centre and drove home to clean up what was slowly becoming our unrecognizable life. I braced myself for the week ahead: I was moving into a newly promoted role at work while caring for our kids alone, worrying about Robert's wellbeing, and no mom for support but instead needing to be hers. I felt completely isolated and had more on my plate than I could handle.

And then I was served up some more.

While my husband was away with no contact, I learned from my daughter's pediatrician that she had severe scoliosis and would need to wear a body brace for 20-hours a day for the next three years with the possibility of needing spinal fusion surgery. My daughter is a competitive dancer – dancing was her life. Taking it all in, I was brought to my knees.

I went from having a daily interactive relationship with my energetic mom, in which we texted 20 times a day, to a daughter whose mom couldn't even text one line or read the draft of the first book she published – let alone any books for my mom's pleasure. From a marriage that I thought of as the most secure and loving partnership and parenting duo, to a wife whose husband was in rehab for alcoholism. And then, most painfully, I was no longer the mom of three healthy kids. My 12-year-old daughter had years of difficult treatment ahead of her at a most fragile age with no guarantees of avoiding life-altering surgery.

And then there was everyday life of course. I still had my demanding career and the natural circus that is your world when you have three hormone-raging teens under one roof. With the weight of three health crises on my heart, suddenly the hiccups of life started to feel like too much. Things like my eyebrow being burnt off during a waxing appointment (don't ask – I don't know), my eldest son being diagnosed with a heart murmur and being taken off medication he needed, my car getting stuck in a snow bank with no way to pick up the kids, another son getting pushed through a window at school, and losing my wallet… Let's just say I wasn't in the best shape.

At first, I spent my days unfocused at work and struggled to keep my head above water. I went from being at the top of my game to crying at my desk. I would cry myself to sleep at night thinking of my husband's pain and of not being able to contact him to tell him about our daughter's health. I would constantly wonder what would happen to my daughter and my mother's lives. Suddenly, it seemed we had lost so much of what I had been trying to build all my life: a healthy, happy family that I could protect from all the bad things and surround with all the good ones.

That all lasted about six weeks, and then I decided to get my shit together. No, I couldn't change what happened, but I could take back power over my life and my role as their lighthouse.

Choose. Act. Become.

Under the bubbles in my tub one evening, three simple, powerful words replayed themselves in my head, and I suddenly felt a weight lift off of me. I realized: everything I did and was in my life before

2014 was all I needed to get my family and me through this. No, more than get through it – master it. Make it beautiful. Make it better than before. I realized that the same skills, systems, tools, and mindset I had developed to find happiness in my challenging childhood and find success in my career would be everything I'd need to get my personal life back on track.

I wasn't going to let a brain injury, alcoholism, a body brace and a burnt off eyebrow be the end-all for my vision of a happy family and good life, was I? Most certainly not. And so, I chose "beautiful above all" as the mantra that ruled this next chapter of our lives. I sat for hour upon hour and determined all of the actions I would take to support this vision. And then I would live into the person I would need to become to ~~handle~~ master all that became our family's truth.

The next few months were a blur. We ordered in a lot, I never blow-dried my hair, and our kitchen was piled high with dishes. I wasn't an attentive friend during those times and maybe didn't remember birthdays. I gave up exercise and slept less. Our snow didn't get shovelled, so our mailman couldn't deliver the mail. I made many personal calls at work for support and didn't try for the newest promotion. I didn't watch my favorite TV shows and didn't sweep my kitchen floor. What I did do was laser-focus on my mom's health, my husband's delicate recovery and return home, the banding together of our family, and getting my dancing girl into a gruelling three years of wearing a body brace 20-hours a day. I researched and communicated, strategized and reached out. I got heavily involved in what was most important to me from every single angle that I could think of. I became my own version of Superwoman, with crazy hair and a dirty home.

In those months, I became everything I was ever meant to be in my life.

"Everything is figure-outable," as Marie Forleo says.

And she is right.

My goals required me to stretch my abilities. I wanted to make our lives even more beautiful than they were before, my marriage even stronger, my mother-daughter relationship even more supportive, and my daughter's life filled with even more beauty and freedom. I was going to make our lives as beautiful as I had always intended – this I knew for sure.

Today, five years later, our lives are just that. And while they are also filled with the realities of post-concussion syndrome, recovery from alcoholism, and scoliosis, I have also never been happier or felt more at peace. I am even more clear on what matters to me and what needs to be done to sustain such a life, riding its unpredictable waves and all. Our family is closer than ever, our relationships are more authentic, our friendships more supportive, and our careers more rewarding and abundant than I had ever believed could be possible. "Weather doesn't matter," I have always said, but now I truly understand what this means.

All my adult life, friends and clients have asked me, "How do you do it, Tarina?" I held a successful leadership role at a global pharmaceutical company on a part-time basis while sustaining my own business the other two days a week. I did this for 13 years, after which point I left my corporate role to focus on my entrepreneurial one and within three weeks was up-and-running a full-time performance consulting and executive coaching business, *LifeWorks*. Robert and I built a loving and committed relationship and raised three confident, autonomous, and happy kids whom we are deeply close with. We have a beautiful home in Montreal as well as a cottage on the lake. Robert and I take a minimum of nine weeks off a year and never work on weekends. Most importantly, we have strong relationships with our family and friends. And so when people used to ask me, "What's your secret?" I had many strategies and perspectives to share, but everything truly crystallized in 2014.

And that secret is deliberateness: choosing, acting, and becoming what matters to you, *on purpose*.

It's all about deliberateness. All of it. Every last crumb of it (not swept from my floor!). Now, after 20 years of helping others lead their best lives and after rising from my own family's challenges, I have truly come to discover the formula to personal fulfillment and freedom. The beauty is that deliberateness is free to anyone who chooses this path. Deliberateness can also be learned: I have proven its success over and over again with thousands of people and groups I have worked with, both locally and around the world, from stay-at-home parents to CEOs of global companies. People who work with me (and who are ready to do the work) experience a remarkable life that matters to them.

This book is an invitation to begin your work with me. It will equip you with the mindset and practical tools I have used to create massive change in the personal and professional lives of thousands of people over the course of my career as an executive performance coach, global learning strategist and influencer, leadership trainer of Fortune 500 companies, and as a wife and mom of three.

The story I've shared is mine, but you have yours – your own unique, beautiful, messy, awesome story. You are the hero of your own life and it is my honor to be your guide over the course of this next conversation. My vision for its unfolding is to ensure that you know you are the writer of your story and to empower you with all that you need to lead a remarkable, authentic life, no matter the weather or demands of the modern world.

I am excited to see you begin to create, truly love, and appreciate every day of your remarkable life. I want it for you, and I can taste it for you.

This is your one life as *you* – it's *yours*.

Live it without regrets.

Live it deliberately.

Let's do this.

With gratitude,

Tarina

CHOOSE WHAT MATTERS

GAINING CLARITY AND SETTING YOUR VISION

"Destiny is not a matter of chance. It is a matter of choice.
It is not a thing to be waited for, it is a thing to be achieved."

– William Jennings Bryan

THE ONLY BOSS THAT REALLY MATTERS

- 1 -

Let's start off with something that surprises most people who know me: I was raised by total hippies. My mom met my dad in college in Montreal – she was a 19-year-old student and he was her professor – and, one year later, I was born. It was the '70s, and despite the changing times, I grew up in what was then considered a not so conventional household. Our family was blended, made up of my two brothers from my dad's previous marriage and me. For the first few weeks of my life, my parents considered having me sleep in a drawer as a makeshift bassinet. They were unmarried (which I only learned 20 years later!), as they felt their love was above needing the whole legal thing. They must've also felt they were above needing to drive, because neither of them did that, either. Evenings were spent with their friends, who gathered at our house to talk all things philosophy and culture late into the night. Most unconventional feeling, though, was the fact that my dad was mentally ill. They called it depression, though we later learned that he had been misdiagnosed and suffered from manic depression with personality disorders. In our free-spirited, discussion-loving household, this was our Everest:

the topic we could talk 'til the sun came up but never addressed how to climb. I loved the openness but craved the equipment to deal with the terrain.

My dad's illness increased in severity as each year passed, and by the time I was 10, I found myself living with the expectation that bad things could strike at a moment's notice. I sought refuge in the homes of friends, where stability and ease seemed the norm for them but a luxury for me. Don't get me wrong – there was a great sense of security and playfulness in my home, provided by my mom's boundless, overflowing love. She gave me every ounce of affection and care she had, which provided me with a great deal of peace. But even so, even with all that love, I craved a compass to guide me. This feeling persisted, and by 15-years-old I felt as though I was weaving through a hazy maze, unattended and entirely responsible for forging my own path. I was always asking myself, "What's the plan?" I wanted the many good things to stick around and all the bad ones to go away and recognized that no one else seemed to be accounting for how to do this.

Why am I telling you this?

Because through this experience I learned that the only way to know the plan was to create one myself. I learned something that I believe is the fundamental difference between the people who are deliberate and fulfilled, and those who aren't. And it all comes down to this question: do you hold an internal or external locus of control? In other words:

Are you the boss of your brain or do you practice puppet brain?

For all you psych majors out there, the term "locus of control" is probably old news. But whether or not you're familiar with the concept, hear me out because it will make the difference between getting a little or a lot out of this book, between staying right where you are or moving closer to the beautiful, deliberate life you're seeking.

Locus of control boils down to whether you attribute your successes and failures to your own decisions and behaviour (internal) or to the behaviours and happenings in your environment (external). People with an internal locus of control tend to feel a greater sense of personal responsibility than those with an external locus – who look to their surroundings to explain their reality. The honest truth is that there are pros and cons to both approaches, though the research says that people who bear an internal locus of control are generally more self-confident, less anxious, and more empowered than those who believe their lives are at the mercy of their environment.

Here are a couple of examples of each locus at play in daily life:

1. You receive the annual award for outstanding contribution in your department at work.

Someone with an internal locus of control might think, *Heck yes! I worked my butt off, poured my heart into it, and my work is being recognized. Go, me!*

Someone with an external locus of control would likely believe, *What luck! Thank goodness that star Sandra transferred departments or I'd never have stood a chance.*

Or

2. You didn't receive the annual award for outstanding contribution in your department at work.

Someone with an internal locus of control might think, *Too bad! I worked hard but probably not smartly enough. Time to review my process and learn from it so that next time I'm better equipped.*

Someone with an external locus of control might reason, *Go figure. I didn't have enough guidance from my manager. How was I supposed to perform well?*

See the difference?

Boss of your brain (internal locus) versus puppet brain (external locus).

VS

My mom's love and adoration equipped me with the confidence I needed to fully accept responsibility for my life, and at an early age, I decided that I was the boss of my brain, that it was up to me to shape the reality I desired. I realized that when I made a mistake it was my own to learn from, and when I succeeded in something it was the result of how I harnessed my qualities, skills, and determination.

The first section of this book is devoted to choice – to choosing what matters. Doing so lays the foundation for deliberate living: you can't act or become what matters to you before you *know* what matters to you. And this knowing is reflected in the choices you make. But, even before facing these choices, you need to truly believe that you are the boss of your brain. You need to know that, no, you are not a cog in the machine or a slave to your responsibilities; **you are the master of your life.** You may feel you don't have a choice in some areas of your life right now, but this is not the case. There is always a choice. It may be a difficult one and the consequences of some choices may be too grave for you to bear, but it is always up to you to decide. This might sound harsh, but really it's a great thing! It means that you are the decision-maker in your life, that you have total agency over your life and your experiences – *if you so choose.*

Being the boss of your brain, adopting an internal locus of control, and accepting responsibility for the life you have and the life you desire is the first and most critical choice you can make. To all those already practicing this: I salute you. It's not always an easy road, and it's tempting to blame others and our circumstances. We need to be kind to ourselves in the process, which is all the time. To those who are only just considering it: I'm here to tell you that that's OK and that you can do it. Change is hard but it's also possible. Sometimes the stakes need to be high before we're willing to do something different, so here's an idea to consider: **be the boss of your brain – your best life depends on it.**

THE STRUGGLE MYTH
AND THE WHEN/THEN MONSTER

-2-

If you're like the majority of us, you've probably been told a thousand times over that if you "work hard" and "do it all" you'll make a good life for yourself. Underlying those fake pearls of wisdom is the message that success only comes to those who struggle through endless work hours that bleed into their weekends, endure little sleep and rest, and generally push themselves to their limit. "The struggle is real," they say, and it's no wonder why.

The real problem is that many of us have already recognized the flaw in this messaging but still buy into it. Think about it: are you working overtime most days? Do you sacrifice your moments of recharging to get that extra bit of work done? Are your colleagues more apt at knowing your favorite lunch order than your spouse is?

Now, let me ask you: why are you doing this to yourself?

When I pose this question to my clients, what comes up in nearly every discussion is the belief that doing so will eventually lead them to a point where they can *finally, totally, fully* enjoy all they've worked for – and they're not talking about retirement!

But when does this point of finally enjoying your life actually kick in? When you have the perfect job, salary, relationship, family, body, etc.? If you believe you need to struggle until everything is "perfect" before you can start enjoying life and being grateful for it, you'll never get there. If you believe the road to joy and freedom is paved with paying dues and distress, you've missed the point. The Dalai Lama summed up this paradox perfectly when he said:

Man... sacrifices his health in order to make money. Then he sacrifices his money in order to recuperate his health. And then he is so anxious about the future that he does not enjoy the present; the result being that he does not live in the present or the future; he lives as if he is never going to die, and then dies having never really lived.

Yikes.

Sadly, I've seen this unfold in the lives of so many wonderful people who work their butts off and never make the time to truly enjoy all the abundance they've earned because they're so busy hustling towards a shinier promise held in the future. They've bought into the Struggle Myth and it's cousin, the When/Then Monster.

Don't know this one?

When I am smart enough, *then* I will apply for that dream job.

When I lose the weight, *then* I will create a dating profile.

When I'm less busy at work, *then* I will spend more time with the kids.

When I have more experience, *then* I will be confident.

When people recognize and appreciate me, *then* I will feel good about myself.

When I organize my garage, *then* I will start that book I've been dreaming about.

The list goes on.

We've all been visited by the *When/Then* Monster before. You'll know it's dropped by when your feelings of desire are cut off just as quickly as they came by limitations steeped in shame and self-doubt, or senseless hesitation and permission-seeking thoughts. What's especially dangerous about this beast is that, in many cases, people never feel that the *when* happens – or if it does, it happens too late – and the *then* passes them by.

When I was in my teens, my dad bought a beautiful soap and gave it to me in a delicate box. This was a rare gesture for him, so it was an especially precious gift. So precious, in fact, that I never opened the box because I was waiting for a special occasion. Well, years went by before I decided the occasion was special enough. It wasn't until my university graduation that I felt justified to use it, but when I opened the box the bar had long melted away. My *When/Then* Monster had taken over and I was left with a *when* (my graduation) but no *then* (enjoying the soap). Now, a melted soap bar isn't a story worth crying over and some things truly are better with time, but this kind of thinking holds far too many people back from doing, experiencing, and becoming what and who they want. So let me tell you what I tell my clients: the struggle myth is just that, a myth, a false belief that you can choose to abandon as early as NOW. **It's not about doing it all, or only about working hard; it's about doing *what matters to you* and about working *deliberately*.** Take some time to examine your own paradigm about the road to fulfillment. Does it uplift you or weigh you down? Look at your own list of *whens/thens*. Are your whens healthy, realistic goals you're committed to, or have they been influenced by your *When/Then* Monster? How can you get closer to your *thens* today?

In her book *The Writing Life*, Annie Dillard writes, "How we spend our days is, of course, how we spend our lives."

The choice is up to you.

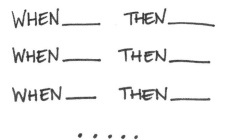

WHAT L'OREAL GOT RIGHT

-3-

In 1971, L'Oreal Paris came out with one of the most legendary slogans of all time. You know the one I'm talking about:

"L'Oreal Paris: because I'm worth it."

Since its first appearance, the slogan-turned-mantra has undergone several reworks – from "I'm worth it," to "you're worth it," to "we're worth it". Point is:

I'm worth it.

You're worth it.

We're (all) worth it!

Hardly a mouthful and yet so hard to swallow. Why is that?

It doesn't matter if I'm speaking with a CEO or a university student, time and again the same fears come up when people wrestle with their self worth, and they sound something like this: "I'll mess it up." "I don't trust myself." "Who am I to be visible?" At one point or another they bought into the ideas that they aren't allowed to make mistakes, aren't capable of doing/handling it, and aren't ___ enough to be seen. This isn't uncommon. In fact, this is far too common.

What *is* unique is the reason each person decided to adopt these limiting stories in the first place.

In work, if there's a problem causing significant damage or resistance to success, you put your energy into fixing it. And you choose to do this without much deliberation. *How* you fix the problem might require a lot of thought, but the decision to address the issue is a no-brainer. Oddly then, when it comes to beliefs like, "I don't trust myself," so many people accept the problem and move on to something else! Not only do they not think about how to fix the problem, they don't even choose to fix it in the first place. Why? Because it's hard. And painful. And they know it will mean stretching themselves out of their comfort zone, no matter how uncomfortable staying there might be. The problem with this is that if you don't believe you're worth it, every action, reaction, ritual and habit you exercise will speak to that. Not only will you feel it, but so will everyone around you.

The good news is that each moment presents you with the choice to do it differently (and you are the boss of your brain!). For some, this mindset is easier to commit to in the morning with a clean slate. However it may be for you, the important thing is to recognize that **nothing will be as beneficial or impactful in creating your deliberate life as choosing to invest in your self worth.**

So, where do you start?

How to Move from Limiting Beliefs to the "I'm Worth It" Mindset:

1. Call out the limiting belief when it pops into your head. Ask yourself: what is it exactly that I'm telling myself?

2. Consider that this belief might actually be an assumption: is what I'm thinking absolutely true, or is it possible that I am choosing to see it that way?

3. Reflect on the assumption: where did that story come from? At what point did I choose to believe this?

4. Challenge the assumption: how can I reframe this belief so that it serves me and others?

5. Rinse and repeat.

This exercise can feel anything from silly to painful and, eventually, pretty awesome. As my clients go through this process, they usually experience all of these emotions. It may not happen the first time or the 12th, but if you stick with it, the benefits will catch up to you. And it makes sense: you only adopted those limiting beliefs through reinforcement in the first place, so the only way to replace them with empowering scripts is by challenging them every time they pop up!

And let's not forget about your people. I wholeheartedly believe that this process is not one that happens in isolation; you need to find people who believe in you, who will cheer you on, pick you up and celebrate your successes. (We'll talk more about this later in the book.)

You have all the capability you need inside of you and it's quietly waiting for you to harness it. If you mess up, so what? Learn from it! You have it in you to improve and do better the next time. Don't trust yourself? Research the heck out of the thing you're facing, prepare for it, and then try it! Afraid to be visible? Get over yourself! While you're busy worrying about what others think of you, they're busy worrying about what you're thinking of them! (You have no idea how true this is. You would be amazed at how many accomplished people quietly struggle with self worth.)

L'Oreal's slogan celebrated its 40th anniversary last year, and it's because they got something right: not only are we worth it, we all need to believe we are, too.

LIFE AS A PACKED LUNCH

- 4 -

Before making deliberate choices, you need to know where you want to end up. And even before this, you need to know where you're currently at. How do *I* do this? It pretty much comes down to a packed lunch.

Let me explain.

I married my husband Robert when I was 24. He's 12 years older than me, and in our early years, I had the less demanding career, which put me in charge of preparing our lunches throughout the week. The loving new wife that I was, I approached this task with attention and care: fresh, whole grain breads from the bakery, cured meats, tomatoes, pickles, fancy mustards, and sometimes even a handful of alfalfa sprouts if I was feeling especially domestic. I'd slip those gourmet sandwiches in his lunch with cut up veggies, a dollop of hummus, and a love note to brighten his day.

Then baby #1 came along and his lunches took a hit: bread from aisle 10, meat (any kind), with a pickle on the side. A yogurt. Maybe a dessert.

Baby #2 26 months later: a slice of bread and a pack of salami. A jar of mustard and a butter knife. A carrot – unwashed – thrown in.

Baby #3 21 months later: whatever was reaching its expiry date in the fridge, tossed in a bag.

With three kids under the age of seven and an increasingly demanding career, what was once a fun, thoughtful task quickly devolved into a Mouldy Salami Sandwich Situation (MSSS). Robert's assistants still tease me about the obvious decline of his packed lunches in relation to my career and motherhood. When Robert found the mould on that fateful day, he sent a gentle email calmly requesting that I *please* refrain from making his lunches, ever again. And so for me, packed lunches are an important indicator of where I'm at in my life and where my time and energy are going. Theoretically speaking, there's no shame in a MSSS so long as it's a deliberate choice (though I'd say this is going a tad too far). The thing is, deliberateness is a way of life, and it all begins with knowing yourself inside out: your values, strengths, weaknesses, limitations, and where you spend your time and devote your energy.

In short, it begins with knowing what kind of packed lunch you're making and why. What does yours look like today?

IT'S NOT A SCARCITY; IT'S A CHOICE

-5-

If I hear one concern more than any other, it's some variation of *sigh*, "I just don't have enough time". It doesn't matter what the person's roles or responsibilities are – there are never enough hours in a day, or days in a week.

It presents itself in a million different ways, to a million different degrees:

Q: "Can you come to the family reunion?"

A: "I wish I could, but I just can't squeeze it in."

Q: "Will you cheer me on at tonight's soccer game?"

A: "Sorry honey, I'd love to, but I don't think I'll make it."

Q: "Want to join us for drinks after work?"

A: "That sounds great, but I'm totally swamped."

If you're one of these people, I'd like to respectfully call B.S. on this.

Let's look at my own experience for a second. For the past 20 years, I've been running a successful leadership performance consulting and executive coaching business while raising three wildly different, active kids who have grown into three wildly different, active teenagers. I travel at least once a month delivering speeches, executive coaching sessions, and leadership trainings around the world. For 13 of those 20 years I also worked as a leader in Human Resources at a global pharmaceutical company. In addition to these roles, I'm a dedicated wife, daughter, best friend, and mentor. My husband and I own two homes and look after them with our family. I *also* take a minimum of nine weeks off per year and haven't worked on weekends since Robert and I got married 22 years ago (that was actually part of our commitments to each other!).

It's not that my life is any less demanding than most people's, it's that I view and use time differently than they do.

It's All in Your Head

The belief that there isn't enough of something and that there never will be is called a **scarcity mindset**. Adopting this mindset is at best uncomfortable and at worst dangerous, often serving as the silent motive behind nasty feelings like greed, competitiveness, and straight-up fear. There's good news and bad news when it comes to this: the good news is that your scarcity mindset is, as the name indicates, all in your mind. The bad news is that there couldn't be a worse place for it to be! Whether or not the thing you're after is truly in shortage is almost inconsequential. So long as you perceive it to be the case, your experiences will reflect this belief and you will act accordingly.

Just like puppet brain, the struggle myth, or flawed beliefs of self worth, a scarcity mindset is something you choose to take on at some point in your life, oftentimes without realizing you're doing so. And I get it! Messages of scarcity bombard us every day – it's the basis of modern commerce. The less we feel we have, the hungrier we are for it. The important thing to remember is that time is not just about quantity, it's about quality too.

A New Perspective

Joyful, fulfilled people rarely look at life through a lens of scarcity. Instead, they operate according to the theory of abundance: the idea that **there is more than enough** and always will be. One way to consider this is that **time is the ultimate equalizer** – everyone has the same amount of it. Unlike money or even recognition, no one in this world has more hours in a day or a week than anyone else. Of course, having more money or fame generally means having more options, like hiring help to free up time, but the fundamental principle remains, which is that we're all dealing with the same calendar week, and we're all capable of making choices. (Note: when it comes to seeking help, it's not all about money. Before I had much of it, I would barter services to help get things done. In fact, I still barter to this day! There's always a way.) So when I listen to my clients express their dissatisfaction in their lack of time, I nod my head and then ask them if they know what this means:

168

Do you know what it represents?

If you don't, that's a strong sign that you may not be consciously choosing where you spend your time. The number 168 represents the total number of hours each of us has in a week. Author Laura Vanderkam breaks this down in her book, *168 Hours: You Have More Time Than You Think*. I refer to 168 hours when talking about time because it's not only about management but also about perception. Most of my clients have never thought about time in this way and are amazed when we examine their time use in these terms.

Together, we look at:

1. Where are they choosing to spend their time?

In order to really get this right, I ask them to write down what they spend their time doing every hour for a week, from when they wake up to when they go to sleep. We look at all aspects of their time use, from recreation to work, relationships to finances and beyond. And you know what? People are always amazed at how much time they're misusing! And how much time they actually have! When I did this with a client recently she realized that she was mindlessly spending 25 hours a week on social media. Twenty-five hours!

Most clients also realize just how inefficient they actually are while at work. Again, time is not just about quantity, it's about quality. It's about how we actually use our time, how productive and intentional we are with it, and how those decisions make us feel.

2. Are they satisfied with these choices?

In other words, do these choices connect to their most important values and priorities? Think about my client who was spending 25 hours a week on social media. If this was something that made her feel great and was an important way for her to connect with her friends, whom she highly values, maybe those 25 hours would be considered well spent. But that wasn't the case. In fact, doing this left her feeling totally depleted, irritated, and envious. It wasn't something that recharged her for the rest of the week, it actually sucked her energy and took away from time she could otherwise spend with her family – one of her highest priorities.

How to Take Ownership of Your Time

1. Take note of what you do every hour (or every half-hour if you can) for a week. Do your best; if you fall short you'll still get some great insights. Keep it simple but be totally honest. Remember: this is for you.

2. Review your 168 hours and mark one of the following next to each activity you noted down: Energized you (E), Drained you (D), and Wasted your time (W). Note: We will be looking at the concept of energy more deeply in the next chapter, but this is a good place to start.

Once you begin looking at how you're spending your time on a granular level and examine how it makes you feel, you'll be better equipped to make deliberate choices about what you want to do with it. As a general rule, try removing all activities that you deem as time-wasters, delegate or minimize activities that drain you, and use the freed-up time for activities that give you energy.

Planning to Live in the Moment

My BFF Leah told me that if I was to write a second book, it should be on how to plan to live in the moment. I thought that was an interesting phrase, because so often people associate planning with rigidity and living in the moment with spontaneity – the two don't exactly go together. What I love about this concept though is that it's totally true: through deliberate planning and time management, I'm left with a whole lot of time to do whatever I want! (I refer to this as "anything/anytime" in my agenda, which gives me a time slot of carte blanche.)

Some people are turned off by the idea of time management. I imagine they picture people like me as robots with alarms ruling our lives. But the whole purpose of actively managing time is to give myself an abundant amount of time for the things that matter to me, including spontaneous activities. Taking inventory of our time, examining how it's making us feel, and then planning to live in the moment, makes all the difference between going to the family reunion or not, watching your kid's soccer game firsthand or only hearing about it later, and connecting with your peers or feeling like the odd one out.

Time: it's not a scarcity; it's a choice.

What will you choose to do with your 168?

GOT FUEL?

-6-

Meet Mike: Mike's a 32-year-old travelling salesman, so naturally, he's on the road a lot. After a long day of meetings, Mike jumps in his car and starts to head home. He's about two hours away when he gets a call from his buddy Phil, who tells him that a group of friends are getting together to watch the hockey game at their local pub and invites him along. The game starts in an hour so Mike's sure to be late, but he figures he could use some unwinding and happily agrees. Ninety minutes later, a symbol illuminates on Mike's dashboard: he's almost out of fuel. He keeps his eyes peeled for a service station along the highway and takes the nearest exit. The detour is annoying – he's eager to get there and relax – but soon enough he's back on his way. He arrives later than expected but is warmly greeted with a pint and enjoys a relaxing evening.

Not much to this story, right?

Didn't have the climactic moment you were expecting?

That's because when the "empty" sign lit up on Mike's dashboard, he did the thing we would *all* do: he refuelled his car. There was no drama, and all was well.

No one would consider driving on empty. If Mike kept going despite the warning signs, eventually his car would have come to a full stop and he would have been stuck on some highway, alone, in the dark. Not only would his evening have been ruined, but his next day would likely have been affected as well.

Why am I telling you this? Because most people take better care of their cars than they do themselves! When a light goes off in your car, you might be able to ignore it for a while, but pretty soon you're giving it what it needs, right? And if you don't know what it needs, you look up the symbol in the manual, and if that leaves you more puzzled than before, you call an expert for help. It's simple enough to understand and apply in this context, but difficult for many to commit to when it comes to refuelling and caring for themselves.

We can't run on empty. Sooner or later, it catches up to us and we start missing out on what's important to us, we start ruining our days, our weeks, our months, and our years. We try to run marathons but don't know how to recover from them. Years ago, one of my colleagues and the co-author of our book, *More Life, Please!* Dr. Christian Marcolli of Marcolli Executive Excellence explained to me that it's not just about managing your time, it's about managing your energy. He said that, contrary to the marathon concept, the most productive and happy people are those who sprint and recover, sprint and recover. This means giving whatever you're doing all you've got with a clear end in sight and then re-energizing afterwards. The key is to know how to recover, to know what fuels you and what drains you. Without knowing this it's impossible to prioritize your time in ways that nurture you and reflect your needs.

Life demands so much. If you don't balance out the energy-suckers with the energizers, you'll be living your life on that dark, isolated highway, and nobody wants that! So if you're not refuelling already, it's time to start. But first, let me address a common barrier: the idea that re-energizing is a selfish act. Re-energizing is not selfish. In fact, not doing so is taking away from the important things in your life and the lives of those around you. It's simple: **if you aren't energized, you have nothing left to give**. If you have nothing to give, then you can't be of service to others. And if you try to give when you're on empty, dangerous things like resentment, distrust, poor health, and failed relationships can result. On the other hand, when we discover what fuels us, what gets us "in the flow" as many call it, life becomes so much richer, more joyful, and vibrant. And that's what deliberate living is all about.

You might already have a good idea of what gives you energy and what sucks it. If you do, make sure that when you're looking at those 168 hours of yours there's a designated place for doing more of the things that fuel you and less of the things that drain you. For example, about 20 years ago I learned that one of the most important ways for me to re-energize is through surrounding myself in nature. I was blessed to marry a man who had a family cottage and quickly grew reliant on the tranquility, beauty, and disconnect cottage living could provide. (Mind you, sleeping in a tent in my backyard under the stars largely has the same effect on me.) As soon as I realized how energizing this was for me – and I was lucky my husband feels the same way – our family made cottage weekends our biggest priority. Six years ago we took the plunge and bought our own cottage, which we named Trent. Despite three busy kids, despite Robert and I having demanding careers, despite home and family obligations, despite boys who wanted to play hockey and a daughter who dances competitively, we make sure to spend as many weekends at Trent as possible. This has meant leaving the city at 11pm on Friday nights so the kids can still hang with their friends, only going up for one night if Emma has a competition that weekend, and other compromises as the kids become more independent. Still, there is rarely a weekend when we don't go up, because we know that's what we need in order to be at our best for the rest of the week.

Finding what energizes you should be a fun process, and it doesn't require you to have luxurious things, either. In fact, when I work with clients to discover what energizes them, most often it's the simplest of things that do the trick. And it starts with one request: **think of the last time you felt deeply happy and full of life.** So many people haven't considered this! I remember asking this of a client who came to me feeling really unsatisfied and grouchy. When she started thinking about my request, tears filled her eyes and her entire demeanour changed. In an instant, she became a softer person. I thought she was going to share a huge moment with me, but instead it was something so simple. She described a time she came home after work and looked out the kitchen window and saw her two kids playing in the pool. Instead of merely glancing, she took a moment to really watch and saw them join hands underwater. She thought, "Wow, those are my two kids, and they're playing together". She realized how much happiness such a simple moment brought her and recognized that she needed more time to be present in her life, to not always be inside doing chores but to make time to be out there with her kids.

When was the last time you felt deeply happy and full of life?

Write it in your schedule.

Do more of it.

LIFE IN BUCKETS

- 7 -

If we were to try to distil all the components of your life into one sentence, that would be pretty hard, wouldn't it? That's because there are so many facets to any given person's life, so many roles to play and so many needs and areas to nurture. Without being aware of these components, life can get pretty hectic, pretty quickly. To manage this, I've always visualized my own life in buckets.

Visualizing my life in buckets is how I keep track of everything and enables me to decipher which areas I'm thriving in and which parts could use a little TLC. Not every bucket holds the same amount of importance, but if it makes up a major portion of my life, it earns its place in my doodles. I started using these buckets many years ago and review them at least twice a year. If significant changes are made in my circumstances, I tip one bucket out and replace it with another! Not sure what I mean? Let's have a look:

How to Look at Your Life in Buckets

Do you want to get a clear picture of which areas in your life are on track and which could use some love and attention? Consider sketching out your own life in buckets:

1. Think of the different areas in your life. Some typical ones include work, social relationships, family relationships, personal growth, spirituality and/or religion, finances, health, leisure, romance, and your environment. If there are other major areas of your life, include them in your buckets.

2. Doodle as many buckets as there are areas of your life, and label each one.

3. On the side of each bucket, mark a scale of 0-10, like this. (Or 0, 5 and 10 for simplicity.)

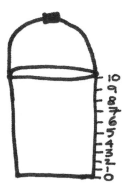

4. Think about how satisfied you are with the area of life your bucket represents. Is it full, empty, halfway?

5. Draw a line of water in your bucket at the level of satisfaction you feel (1-10). For example, if you're really content with your health, your bucket might look like this:

HEALTH

Take a step back and look at all of your buckets. Which are full and which are empty? What are you doing with your full buckets that are making them that way? Can you apply any of those practices to your empty ones?

You can't expect everything in your life to be perfect all at once, so it's normal to have some buckets that are more filled than others. What you don't want are extremes: some buckets overflowing while others are dry as a bone. Above all, what it really comes down to is your highest priorities and values.

BINS 1, 2, AND 3

-8-

Whenever I deliver trainings, I make the joke that I never style the back of my hair, because I'm always facing my audience and have more important things to do with my time before presenting than attempting the impossible (anyone who has tried to style the back of their hair with a blow drier gets the struggle). People crack up every time, but this joke actually reflects something I'm extremely serious about: *setting priorities.*

Your buckets provide you with a snapshot of how satisfied you are in the different areas of your life, but they don't help you gain clarity on exactly what it is you value most. Establishing your priorities is absolutely critical for living deliberately, because it serves as the foundation from which all other decisions can then be based. That's where Bins 1, 2, and 3 come in.

This is a tool I use with absolutely everyone I can get my hands on. It is so fundamental to how we move through the world, be it in our personal or professional lives, that there is never a person who couldn't benefit from using it. Of all the tools that I present and teach to clients, this is the one that usually speaks the most to people.

Bins 1, 2, and 3 can be used for the following purposes:

- Establishing priorities in your overall life.
- Establishing priorities in the buckets of your life.
- Determining priorities when facing a specific problem or big decision.

How to Organize Your Own Bins 1, 2, and 3

Note: You can use this tool for any of the purposes mentioned above, but let's use the example of establishing priorities in the buckets of your life. If you'd like to apply this tool to either of the alternative options – which I highly encourage – do so in the same way as described here.

1. Take one of the buckets of your life and reflect on some of the values and expectations you currently hold for that bucket. Ex: If the bucket you're looking at is health, you might consider values such as exercise you do or don't care to do, the foods you eat, and the amount of water you consume daily. Write these values and expectations down.

2. Now it's time to get clear on priorities. To do this, envision each value and expectation as a physical item taking up space in your life. You want to get organized, so you sort through your items and put each one into one of three bins: Bin 1, Bin 2, or Bin 3. Which bin do you choose for each value and expectation?

Bin 1 – small: They say good things come in small packages, so Bin 1 is the smallest and contains your highest-value items. These are the values of greatest importance to you and are largely non-negotiable.

Ex: In the bucket of health, perhaps one of your Bin 1 items is to "Exercise at least once a week." This is something that, no matter what, you do your very best to uphold because without it you feel as though something is greatly imbalanced in your life.

Bin 2 – medium: This is your medium-sized storage, the kind that contains important enough things that you keep it in the house but don't look though it every day. Everything in this bin is negotiable: nice to have and sometimes will, but also won't focus on all the time.

Ex: Here you might include "Eat organic fruits and vegetables." You'd like to have them if possible and reach for the organic option if it's right there in the grocery store, but it wouldn't bother you too much if you did otherwise.

Bin 3 – large: We may as well call this one the garbage bin, because you're completely willing to let go of these items. It's those things you're not ready to put your energy into, at least for now. It's also the biggest and kept the farthest away from your focus.

Ex: An item here might be "Drink 3L of water per day." Even though that would be great in the ideal world, you're deciding to consciously not care about it.

The ultimate goal with your bins is to make:

- Your Bin 1 the smallest (maximum of 5 items).
- Your Bin 3 the largest.

- Your Bin 2 somewhere in the middle.
- Your life a whole lot simpler.

Thinking about your priorities in terms of Bins 1, 2, and 3 will save you from so much unnecessary anxiety and pain and will replace your troubles with clarity and confidence. Being clear on your (few) top priorities will also provide great direction to your life. Note: The priorities you set should be specific and should ideally be written as behaviours or as action verbs.

Here are some examples of mine to help you get your bins on their way:

Tarina's Big Picture Bins: Parenting My Teenage Kids

Bin 1: Need to have

- Are safe in cars (no drugs or alcohol).
- Spend lots of quality time with family; keep our family close and together.
- Are confident and autonomous.
- Go to university and study something they love.
- Come to the cottage often.

Bin 2: Nice to haves

- Don't swear too often.
- Respect curfews.
- Do chores well.
- Receive high marks.
- Don't roll their eyes and be disrespectful.
- Put cell phones away during homework and night time.
- Let me follow them on social media.

Bin 3: Let go (at least for now)

- Remove wet towels from floor.
- Choose friends I think are a good influence.

- Clean up kitchen in morning.
- Eat all the food in their lunches.
- Keep their rooms clean.
- Listen to music I approve of.
- Keep sibling peace (no rivalry).
- Save hyper-ness for out of the house.
- Play video games I approve of.
- Wear their pants more than once before putting them in the laundry.
- Put towels that they've used to kill flies in laundry and not back on kitchen rack (yup, this happens).

You can't do it all, but you can do all that matters to you if you first choose to gain clarity on exactly what it is that matters to you *most*.

HOW TO PREDICT YOUR FUTURE

-9-

In 2010, I was working two part-time jobs: one as a Human Resources leader, the other as an entrepreneur with an executive coaching and leadership business. I loved my work and life was good, but something inside of me felt I had not yet tapped into my potential as a businesswoman, wife, and mother. One afternoon, I attended a training session on transformational leadership with my Human Resources team and was absolutely blown away by the speaker. Being in HR, you see a lot of trainings and trainers. Many are good, but this man was different. He was whip-smart, warm as anything, and had the whole room beaming. After the training was over I knew I needed more of him. I was intimidated by the thought of asking if he would coach me, but I made the choice that it was what I needed to do and went for it.

His name is Robert Shereck (R. Shereck) of Legacy Transformational Consulting Inc., and, for the last eight years, he has been an exceptional coach, mentor, and friend. He's the guy who taught me how to predict my future.

Predicting your future is simpler than you might think. In fact, the initial process is so simple that when he first proposed it to me I was resistant; I thought it was commonplace and standard. But he was adamant and I trusted him, so I sucked it up and went for it. Before I show you what he taught me, however, let's do a quick recap. By now we've covered some ground, including how you choose to view your:

- Locus of control.
- Path to fulfillment.
- Self-worth.
- 168 hours.
- Energizers and energy-suckers.
- Buckets of life.
- Bins 1, 2 and 3.

The deliberate choices you make in these areas of your life constitute the very foundation of it. **When we begin to truly understand that we shape our reality and are able to clearly identify what we want that reality to look like, life gets really fun.** That's where this exercise from R. Shereck comes in. It's taking our stated values, priorities, and self-knowledge and turning them into goals.

The way it's done is the special part:

How to Predict Your Future

1. Considering what's important to you, take some time to write down the things you deeply want for yourself. They don't have to seem realistic or at all plausible – let yourself really play with your imagination and dreams. Don't hold back. Jot them down.

2. Take these ideas and weigh them up to your buckets and Bin 1 items: are they authentic to your highest priorities and values? Are you willing to stretch yourself to do the

work to attain them? Again, it doesn't matter how possible or impossible they may seem. In fact, the more ambitious, the better! Far too many people only create goals they're sure they can accomplish.

3. Write out these ideas in the form of goals with the following criteria:

- Address each goal in the present tense beginning with "Now that..." followed by how you feel.

- Consider the SMART goal method: Make your goals specific, measurable, actionable, realistic, and timely. (When I say realistic here, I mean respecting fundamental laws, etc. So much more is possible than we allow ourselves to believe!).

- Include as much detail as you can, especially describing how you feel "now that" it's come true.

Ex: Now that I'm running my own online store at 40, serving clients whom I absolutely adore and who inspire me every day, making a six-figure salary in the first year alone and have total flexibility in my daily life, I feel accomplished, empowered, and capable of taking on anything!!!

4. Read these goal statements to yourself often or record yourself reading them and listen to the recording again and again! Allow yourself to get emotionally involved in what it will feel like when those words genuinely reflect your reality. This part is key and brings so much excitement and joy to the process.

I did this exercise about eight years ago and, at the time, felt like a complete phony trying it. Nothing about what I wrote down felt possible; the gap was enormous. In fact, at first I almost felt embarrassed for even acknowledging my desires. But, I put pen to paper and sure enough I had eight specific realities for my future self. At first, I read them every day. I thought of how badly I wanted those things to be true. I would ask myself, "Why *wouldn't* I have this?" "Why am I not allowed to have this?" Then I started thinking in terms like, "If that's my mission, what can I be doing?" Having those concrete visions made doing something about them so much easier.

It took me eight years, but in that span of time I have not only accomplished but I've surpassed seven of my eight goals. (By the time this book is published, I will have accomplished all eight.) I still have that piece of paper, now withered and stained, and refer to it several times a year. What once seemed unachievable is now my life, and as I approach the close of these goals I find myself beginning the process again.

You too can have this same experience, you really can. It all begins with deciding what you want most for yourself.

So, what does your future hold?

REMINDERS, MANTRAS, & THINGS TO KNOW:

You are the boss of your brain.

Happiness is not then, it's NOW. Start today.

You're worth it.

Know what kind of lunch you're packing.

You have more time than you think.

Discover what energizes you and do more of it.

Take a look at the buckets of your life.

Your need-to-haves should be few and

your let-go-ofs should be plenty.

You are your best bet on what your future holds.

ACT
WHAT MATTERS

PLANNING, DOING,
LOVING, AND
STAYING THE COURSE

"Action expresses priorities."
– Mahatma Ghandi

TURNING THE INVISIBLE TO THE VISIBLE

- 1 -

How would you describe yourself? Take a second to really think about this and come up with a handful of descriptions. If I were to ask the people in your life to weigh in, how might their responses compare to yours?

Philosopher Will Durant famously stated, "We are what we repeatedly do. Excellence, then, is not an act, but a habit." My guess is that, like most people, you'd like to think of yourself in high regard and would hope others share your view. And it makes perfect sense: being thought of as a capable, considerate person of integrity plays a critical role in how fulfilling our lives are. As Belgian psychotherapist Esther Perel proclaims, "The quality of our relationships determines the quality of our lives." And the quality of our relationship(s) – with others and with ourselves – is largely shaped by our character. Our character, as Durant lends to, is shaped by our habits, i.e. what we repeatedly do. And our habits are shaped by our actions, which are shaped by our choices.

Are you following me?

The progression looks something like this:

CHOICES
↓
ACTIONS
↓
HABITS
↓
CHARACTER
↓
RELATIONSHIP WITH
SELF
↓
RELATIONSHIP WITH
OTHERS
↓
QUALITY OF OUR
LIVES

Deliberate action and habit building are so much more than simply *getting it done*. They're about integrating our deepest values and intentions into the choices we make and applying them to our lives. In a sense, they're about turning the invisible into the visible. And the visible is ultimately how we come to know ourselves and how others come to think of and remember us.

As you read through this next part, I encourage you to consider your action-taking through the lens of habits. If something resonates with you, think of how to integrate those actions into your everyday life as common practices instead of as once-off efforts. Doing so will increase the overall impact you create for yourself and for others in the long run.

HOLD UP!

Stop right there.

Have you ever had a bad case of the hiccups and then someone jumps out from behind the doorway, shocks the living daylights out of you and finally... the hiccups are gone? The incessant pattern stops. Well, our minds are sort of like that. Sometimes, in order to break our thought patterns to make room for change, we need to be interrup –

Stop it!

Stop proclaiming you're too busy – it's not helping you!

Stop saying your life sucks – fix it!

Stop wishing on birthday candles and start writing vision statements!

Stop assuming your kids' annoying habits will just go away and find proper discipline methods while they're young!

Stop worrying about how you look in photos and get into those photo-worthy moments with your family!

Stop sleeping with your phone beside your bed and buy an old fashioned alarm clock!

Stop saying there's no time to take a vacation from work – organize your schedule and make it happen!

Stop saying you can't meet that deadline – stop talking about it and just do it!

Stop looking at your thighs rubbing together and start focusing on your beautiful eyes!

Stop saying you have no time to have dinner with your family and just go home and eat with them!

Stop thinking the world will cease to turn if you don't have notifications on your phone 24/7!

Stop dreaming of that job and start developing the necessary skills!

Stop making excuses and start taking the action needed to live your one wild and beautiful life!

You can do it.

WHAT MUST BE TRUE?

- 2 -

My daughter is a dancer. Be it ballet, hip-hop, or contemporary form, that girl has been on the move since she could walk. When dancing, Emma's in her zone: focused, nourished, beautiful.

You know the expression, "When it rains, it pours"?

Well, it poured. Hard.

January 2014 saw me at my weakest: with Robert in rehab, my mom suffering from a chronic (albeit relatively mild) brain injury, Nicholas with a prescription complication and a new project on my plate at work, I had become a shell of myself. In the span of three months, my reality turned upside-down and my two most treasured confidantes – my husband and my mom – were virtually absent without any reassurance they would return to me as they once were. So when the doctor called my office to inform me of Emma's diagnosis, I fell apart. "Severe scoliosis," he said.

But my daughter is a dancer.

My first reaction was to go to the bathroom, lock myself in a stall, and cry. To the poor person who walked in that day and listened to my story: thank you. When I got home, I was still too much a wreck to spill the news to Emma. How could I tell her she may not be able to dance? How could I take movement away from my girl when it gave her so much? I went to bed and cried through the night, and in the morning, I decided I needed to get a handle on myself before telling her. Over the following two weeks, I learned everything I could about scoliosis. Novels were replaced with research articles; chats with friends were swapped out for phone calls with experts. By the close of those weeks, my concerns remained but I had decided on one thing: this experience, no matter how challenging, would also be a beautiful one for my girl.

I told Emma the news at our cottage. Like me, she retreated and spent hours crying alone. When the time felt right I approached her with an invitation to join me in the Jacuzzi to discuss a plan of action. I shared my commitment with her: this experience was going to be beautiful. We talked about what that meant to her and together decided on all the ways we had the power to make the experience positive, despite the inevitable challenges.

Making Emma's Experience in a Brace Beautiful

Planned:

- Shopping spree before and after going into brace. ✓

- Throw a "We Have Your Back" empathy party, in which ✓ each of Emma's friends wear her brace for five minutes and learns about scoliosis.

- Perform at the pharma company I worked at in and out ✓ of her brace to show others that she could do anything.

- Get involved with The Scoliosis Foundation. ✓

Unexpected:

- Won an award from The Scoliosis Foundation.
- Became the poster child for her athletic brace.
- Got interviewed on camera for resilience on wearing a brace (and dancing in it).

Were those four years challenging? Absolutely. But they were, as we had intended and planned, also beautiful.

How did we make that happen?

More importantly, how can you make your visions a reality?

With energy, focus, and by answering this question: what must be true? In other words: **in order for your vision to come to fruition, what factors must precede it to make it so?** For Emma, we decided her vision would be to experience life in a brace as beautifully as possible, to leave the situation with more than she went in with. Instead of meeting the circumstances with a bleak perspective – no matter how easy that was to do – we imagined what the best-case scenario would look like and then strategically laid out all of the factors we could control that would need to be realized in order for that vision to become a reality.

It's been one-and-a-half years since Emma's stopped wearing her brace. Ten months ago, we received an update that, despite her dedication, her spine has continued to curve. This means my dancing girl, a girl who has won solo and group competitions over and over again in front of hundreds of people, who has devoted nearly all her life to movement, will be getting spinal fusion surgery, changing her life with the insertion of two rods and 18 screws in her back. This one's been tough to come to terms with, but once we get that surgical date, I'll be inviting her back into the Jacuzzi for our next game plan.

Think about a goal or vision you have for your own life. If it were to become a reality, what list of steps or factors would need to have occurred in order for it to be so? Of these, which do you have control over?

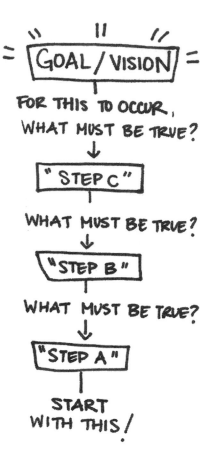

LOVE IN ACTION

-3-

Of all the buckets, bins, and visions we put into action, perhaps none is more important than those concerning love. The number one reason I see torn-apart families, broken friendships, and damaged work relationships is because people lead with the misconception that simply caring about the other person is enough. You've likely heard the saying, "love is a verb, not just an feeling" before, yet the message behind this phrase often escapes people in the bustle of their lives.

Love in action is exactly what it sounds like: taking the love and care you feel inside – the invisible – and transforming it into the visible through actions that are meaningful to your receiver. It's not enough to solely put your personal visions and goals into action, you also need to show those you care about that their visions, goals, and values matter to you as well. Love in action is the consistent process of ensuring that the people around you understand your devotion to them and evaluating how well you're achieving that goal.

We humans are deeply social creatures who need meaningful connection with each other in order to thrive. And yet, relationships are often the first area people take for granted! Why does this happen?

Here are the top reasons I've heard:

1. "They don't need _____, they *just know* how I feel."
2. "I'm really busy and they understand that. Besides, not doing _____ won't go noticed or even make a difference in the long run."
3. "It would be great to show my care but it just takes so much time and effort."

These beliefs are not only bogus, they're also robbing people of reaching new depths of fulfilment and joy in their everyday lives and the lives of those around them!

I worked with the president of a company who frequently spoke about how grateful he was for his employees. In one of our conversations, I asked him, "How are you actually showing them the way you feel?" He was taken aback by the question and realized that, in fact, aside from pats on the back and congratulatory emails, he wasn't truly conveying his appreciation for the devotion of his staff. Together, we brainstormed ideas and he ultimately decided to give away "One Day Off" coupons to all of his employees, enabling them to spend a day with someone who was as important to them as they were to him. The only condition was that, after their day off, they were meant to share how they spent it. Not only were his employees touched by this gesture, but they also began to connect more meaningfully with my client through conversations sparked by sharing their stories with him.

Did this act take a lot of time or effort? Some for sure, but the feedback and benefits that resulted were more rewarding that he had even anticipated.

Oftentimes, love in action is a series of simple gestures and rituals – the continuous sunshine and showers required to keep our precious relationships nourished and strong. Sometimes, though, life challenges us to rise to new occasions. And when it does, we too must raise our efforts for loving.

The greatest gestures of love in action in my own life occurred in January 2017, when I discovered that Robert had relapsed from sobriety. My family and I believed he was going on three years without a drink, but just as we thought we were approaching a milestone, we learned that he had been drinking for the past year-and-a-half. I was devastated: for the drinking, definitely, but more than anything for the secrecy.

I immediately phoned my BFF, Vanessa, for a dose of her wisdom, and in an instant, she came over to talk things through. I decided to cancel everything in my calendar for the week, packed a bag and headed to the cottage for some time to think: *could I ever trust Robert again? Could I stay in our marriage?* I had been totally blindsided. Never in a million years did I anticipate we would face these issues in the first place, never mind a hidden relapse. Even more surprising was that I was honestly asking myself these questions.

In the haze of the days and evenings that followed, my past mentor R. Shereck came to mind. We hadn't spoken in months, but I reached out with an email seeking advice. He replied and asked me to return to my most fundamental values, reminding me that Robert is an amazing man, an incredible father, and a devoted husband…who really needed some help. He said, "I've never met your husband in person, but I want to talk to him on the phone because I really care about you."

I agreed and not long after Robert arrived at our cottage and got on the phone with R. Shereck. They spoke for a few hours. Those hours felt like days. R. Shereck told my husband that, despite his relapse, he was a man of integrity who was in deep need of a transformational course. When we returned to the city, Robert cancelled all of his upcoming business and entered himself into a costly, 14-hours-a-day, three-day course on transformation with his personal goal of living into his integrity. When the course was over, my three kids and I joined him for the closing commitment ceremony. Of the hundreds that participated, five were selected to speak and my Robert was one of them. Now, this is a man who is generally reserved. If I'm the family extrovert, he's our introvert. Despite this, he stood in front of 300 people and spoke for 15 minutes about his struggle, his remorse, his firm commitment to sobriety and, most importantly, his promise to always be honest with our family. I've never seen my sons cry so much in their lives. People approached Robert after the ceremony to share a hug and words of encouragement and admiration. I decided that day that I 100% trusted that he would communicate with me about everything, no matter what. When I followed up with R. Shereck he asked, "Have you actually told Robert that you totally trust him and believe he's capable? When the time is right, I want you to look into his eyes and tell him this in front of your children." And so, the next week I gathered Robert and our three kids together in our living room and performed a "Declaration of Trust" ceremony. I held my husband's hands, looked into his eyes and told him that he had all of my trust, that I believed he would always be honest with me moving forward about the struggles of recovery, and that I held him wholly capable to live up to his commitment of truthfulness. I also gave him a keychain that said "Trust100" as a reminder of his strength and of my belief in him.

From the darkest point in our marriage emerged a partnership stronger than I have ever known. I didn't just get Robert back after our ceremony, I got a Robert who had been touched by the love of those who had extended themselves to him when he really needed it. Along with the impact of his course and ongoing support groups, the displays of belief in and love for Robert shifted the way he viewed himself, which was a key part in his recovery process. Not only have we become closer as partners, but our children have also grown closer with us and each other, too.

I share this story with you because it's a testament to the power of love in action. Even in the most challenging of times – even when facing some of our most difficult decisions – **there is little that the love of others can't do to help us find our own strength**. Vanessa's presence at the drop of a hat gave me the support I needed to realize my next steps. My mentor's gift of time, listening, and guidance gave me the clarity to move ahead with openness and Robert the courage to believe he could face his demons. Robert's public commitment to our family showed us the depths of his devotion and love. The people who spoke with Robert after the ceremony displayed their support and faith. Our Declaration of Trust ceremony was my way of ensuring Robert and our children knew that I was all-in, with a whole heart and total faith. Through a series of love in action, together we built a stronger foundation.

Who are the people you care for most in your own life?

What are the little and big ways you display your love in action to them?

As William James said, "Act as if what you do makes a difference. It does."

SIDEKICKS, LIFESAVERS, AND OTHER TOOLS TO GET 'EM DONE

- 4 -

I have made an entire career out of working with other people's agendas. Clients come to me with the feeling that their lives could be better, and it quickly becomes clear why: **what people do with their time is often gravely disconnected from who they are** (or who they would like to be). Remember your 168 hours? Well, it's not enough to solely analyze how you're spending them – you've got to do something with that knowledge!

You wouldn't take on a project at work without a plan, would you? My guess is that, before blowing the budget and investing your time and energy into it, you would map out a strategy and use certain tools and systems to support the achievement of your objectives. Why would it be any different when it comes to your life? Don't you want more from your experiences?

To keep my world in check and to help others do the same, I use a series of sidekicks and lifesavers. Most of these goodies are actually quite simple, but don't let that sway you. Time and again, they prove to make all the difference.

Want to minimize your anxiety while maximizing your joy and calm?

Give these a go:

Lists

If you couldn't tell already, I'm a bit of a planning junkie. There's nothing I love more than a good list. It can be on your computer or your phone, on Post-It notes or on your chalkboard in the kitchen. The important thing is to get your visions and plans of action down and visible.

People are always amazed at how busy I am while also having so much free time. The solution begins with me taking all those values, visions, and dreams swirling around in my head and getting them onto paper. No one is above a good list, and if more people did them we'd all be a lot less overwhelmed and a lot more focused with our efforts.

With this said, here's a glimpse into my list-making practices:

Weekly To-Do List

Each week I print out a paper with the days of the week on both sides of it. I mark one side as "personal" and the other as "professional". I plan out all tasks here, which gives me a quick and easy glimpse into the week ahead. Anything on this weekly to-do list that isn't crossed off by Sunday automatically makes it onto the following week's list. If a particular task continues to be pushed across weeks, I reassess and see if it's in fact important (Bin 1 material), or if there's no room for it.

Hubby List

My husband gets his own list because he is very special! But seriously, if I leave him to make his own list of what to do around the house… let's just say we'd have lots of gadgets ordered from Costco still sitting in boxes waiting to be set up. He's a great guy but he needs some gentle reminding (ok, severe reminding) in order to hold up his end of our very deliberate life.

So, I manage the home front and provide Robert with a list of things to discuss that week and tasks for him to complete. Then – most importantly – we sit together every Tuesday morning to review and align on it. (Known as Tuesday List Day – so fun! Not.) Similar to my own to-do lists, if Robert doesn't complete something by the following week, we discuss what the barrier was, if it was indeed Bin 1 material or not, and adjust accordingly. This may sound overly formal for a personal relationship, but it works well for us and has made a real difference in the lives of my clients, too.

This tool can be useful for any close relationship, so long as the other person appreciates and sees the value in you delegating for the good of your deliberate lives.

Family/Friend Calendar

If you're part of a couple, have children, or live with a friend, parent, or anyone with whom you need to coordinate schedules and make decisions, a family/friend calendar is a great alignment tool.

To do this, choose one point in the week (usually an evening) and commit to that same day each week. Many people prefer Sunday night, as this helps start the upcoming week off right. With your partner, children, friend, and/or parent, discuss the weekly events and responsibilities, including who will be held accountable: who is where each day, who is picking up whom, what dinners will be together and how food will get made, whose sports and school events are when, what important dates are coming up, etc. With everything determined, print out a page with a weekly calendar on it, fill it in and stick it in a visible place, like on the fridge.

This is a purely logistical meeting that should take no more than 15 minutes but will make the difference between a week of expected craziness or pure chaos.

Note: A great alternative amongst adults is to find a calendar app you can share and plug your plans into. The important part is to get together to review and agree upon all that is in your calendar each week.

Family of Five Functioning Email

Sometimes, a 15-minute meeting isn't enough. That's especially true in the case of my house of five, so I created our not-so-beloved but highly effective "Family of Five Functioning" email.

As if Mondays weren't tough enough, now that our kids are teens I send out an email at the beginning of the week that summarizes all of the upcoming important dates that require each of our presence (think Thanksgiving, birthday celebrations, family time at the cottage, a friend's surgery or difficult time to acknowledge, etc.). With everyone in a hurry at this stage of our lives, this has become the most effective way to communicate key points. (It also allows me to do my nagging in bulk so that for the rest of the week I can focus on our relationships instead of tasks!)

If something isn't working in our family system, it also makes it into the email: "P.S. Please don't leave food on the kitchen floor when you drop it or your sweaty gym bag on my bed." And if something is working especially well, it makes it into the email, too: "Thanks for making the yummy dinner last week, that really helped!" or "Great job not leaving mouldy dishes in your room!"

Fun tip: I hide a trick question in all of these emails (ex. when is Didi's birthday?) that they have to respond to so that I know they read it all and didn't just skim through… Trick of the trade as I got better at this whole thing!

As much as our family calendar and email might not be the thrill of our weeks, we all agree that they leave us feeling clear, aligned, and speaking the same language in our crazy, wonderful family.

DATE: MONDAY

SUBJECT: NAG ALERT!

FROM: MOM

TO: FAMILY OF FIVE

Family Night

One of the most deliberate people I know is my BFF Leah. Everything that girl does is on purpose, and no area is more important to be deliberate in than when it comes to her children. Following her example, years ago I established "Family Night", which is one evening each week that our family comes together so that Rob and I can pass down values and discuss topics with our kids that are important to us. On these nights, we take 20-30 minutes and lead a discussion on a pre-determined topic (anything from drugs to sex to hurricanes to compassion). If we're lucky, we strike a real chord with our kids and they get involved (or at least don't fall asleep!). At worst our kids are a little more aware and know they can talk to us about whatever the topic is if they like. We also curl up on the couch together and watch TED Talks I've saved, or if our kids occasionally play "director", they show us videos they've found interesting or funny. One of the most important aspects of Family Night is that zero logistics or tasks are discussed and we all do our best to not have conflict. I'd say it works 50% of the time, because when they fall asleep I lose it!

What values do you hold that you'd like your kids to adopt? Do you make a conscious choice to display these values? Do you dedicate time to sharing them with your family? Thirty minutes a week is all that's required to get the ball rolling.

Notebooks and Agendas

"There's no place like home," Dorothy of Kansas said. That's also true for all of your lists and preliminary calendars. Enter: notebooks and agendas. If you've made the transfer from paper to digital, that's cool! I'd say about 50% of my clients go for the phone route, while the other 50% prefer paper. The premise is the same for either form of these tools. Point is, you need some way of keeping track of your lists and calendars, while also ensuring:

- You're able to attach a notebook list system either manually or virtually into your agenda.

- You can clearly differentiate work from personal, whether that's through two different agendas or two setups in one agenda that works for you.

- Your agenda captures not just appointments and commitments but also tasks and activities (including leisure time!), present and future.

- Everything in your agenda reflects your values and translates your visions into plans.

My personal favorite is to have a notebook embedded within my paper agenda system, which is in a big courier the size of a small briefcase and includes pockets for extra documents, pens, and business cards. In my notebook/agenda combo I have a week at a glance planner, a month at a glance planner, and a daily planner. Days are divided into two sections: work and home. Doing this is the easiest way for me to keep my lists and calendars organized and in one place. Because of all the buckets in my life, I have tabs in my notebook section that relate to many of them, including:

Tarina's Home Tabs

- My weekly to-do list.
- Each of my three kids.
- My husband (including his Hubby List).
- My mom.
- My BFFs.
- My family calendar.
- Family of Five Functioning notes.
- Each season with related tasks.

Each time in the day or week that I think of something for one of those lists, I flip to the related tab and jot it down immediately: "Talk to Tristan about academic advising" or "Watch __ interview". The same goes for my work tabs:

Tarina's Work Tabs

• My employees and vendors.

• Each key client.

• Each key project.

Using a notebook/agenda combo allows me to reflect on my daily schedule, remember my Bin 1 values and plan them into action, ensure all of my operational tasks get done, and generally monitor how I use my time. More than anything, it takes all of my values and plans out of my head and puts them somewhere concrete, allowing me to rest easy knowing it's all on the page.

Speaking of resting easy, I also double up all of my work appointments and commitments onto my phone calendar to ensure that if – lord forbid – my agenda goes missing, my business is covered. To be perfectly honest, though, if I did lose that baby my life just might be over. Did I mention I was a planning junkie?

Turbo Days

Are there any tasks in your life that overwhelm you just thinking about them? Are there things you've been meaning to do but never get to? If the answer is yes, and if these tasks and to-dos are important to you, you need a turbo day.

TURBO DAY: /'tərbō/ /dā/
WHEN YOU CLEAR YOUR DAY TO FOCUS SOLELY ON ONE TASK THAT'S BEEN NAGGING YOU AND DO THE WHOLE THING FROM START TO FINISH.

Turbo days can mean anything from pulling out all of your family photos and organizing them into albums one day each year, or getting those invoices done and sent out each month. Whatever it is, so long as checking them off is important to you – and not doing so is causing you anxiety – it's time to turbo. Instead of trying to chip away at your task over time, by chunking it into one day, you're not only getting the thing done, you're also minimizing anticipation and the opportunity for neglect and guilt in the process.

This tactic is not only great for specific tasks but also for planning in general. Instead of sprinkling your planning here, there, and wherever you can tuck it in, consider the turbo day approach and select four days a year to do a high-level planning of your work and home lives. Take the time to immerse yourself in your thoughts and reflect on what you really want from the weeks, months, and year ahead. Then it's time to turn to another one of my favorites...

Frontloading

The process of frontloading pulls together the concepts we explored in the first part of this book and applies them to the tools and systems discussed in this chapter. It starts with taking a turbo day to look at the months and year ahead in relation to your energizers, buckets of life, Bin 1 values, and visions. Then it's about pulling out your calendar and marking in the things that matter to you most before anything else, such as the items on your lists or even the items on someone else's list for you.

The truth is, our calendars can get filled up more quickly than we can keep up with sometimes. If we don't ensure that what really matters is planned for and communicated to those involved, it's likely that they'll forever remain invisible aspirations. By frontloading, you ensure that what counts is accounted for.

One of the reasons it's called frontloading is because much of the energy and work is done on the front-end. It takes time, reflection, and strategic planning but pays dividends in the future, as you'll know everything has been considered and your days are filled with the things that truly matter to you.

When working on the corporate side of my executive clients' lives, we plan for frontloading at the beginning of every fiscal quarter. For my own work and home calendars, I choose to frontload four times a year: once in April and October for work, and once in January and September for home life. Friends and family often laugh at me as they get emails in September about Christmas, New Years plans before school has even begun, and pool party invitations while it's snowing in January. They can tease me all they want! Deep down (I think) they wholeheartedly appreciate my frontloading ways, because without them a lot of our social events, celebrations, and travels wouldn't happen. Sure, I can be a pest, but I'm a highly effective one!

To give you a sense of what this looks like before you do your own frontloading, here's a glimpse at some of mine:

Tarina Home Frontloading: September

- Put all kids' days off in calendar and plan lunches with them.
- Book off times kids have final exams to make sure nothing is planned on those weekends.
- Book their doctor and dentist appointments according to their schedules.
- Plan Family Night evenings and dinners for all of us together each week and month.

Tarina Home Frontloading: January

- Put in all days off, weeks off, and travel vacations.
- Plan events for year with all good friends and family.
- Plan family and couples' weekends.
- Put all birthdays in calendar, including when to celebrate and send gifts.
- Plan self-development workshops and couples' workshops.
- Transfer my Bin 1 values and vision statements into actionable, doable items per month or season.

Tarina Work Frontloading: April

- Plan budgeting for fiscal year.
- Plan for strategic projects in Q3 (quarter 3).
- Do cross check on yearly activities.
- Business development for the year – plan key offsite meetings.
- Marketing and branding strategy planning.

Tarina Work Frontloading: October

- Plan performance appraisals.
- Objective-setting development for team.
- Plan 1-1s for direct reports.
- Take yearly objectives of current year and measure success and action items not yet done.
- Predict income following year.
- Review learning objectives accomplished by me and my team.

Have a look at your year as a blank slate.

What are your turbo projects?

What can you frontload that will have the most impact?

The Key to Success

If we look back at our sidekicks and lifesavers, you'll notice a common component strung throughout them, and that's communication. Unless you live in a silo, the majority of your plans will be tied to others in some way. In order for those plans to be realized, you'll need the alignment and collaboration of those involved.

Remember my Tuesday List Day with Robert and my nagging Monday emails? Those are ritualized communication systems that allow our family to go from great on paper to great in real life. You can put anything in place, but it's through communicating – and, even better, through ritualizing the communicating – that you can make your plans a success. By having check-in points, you're able to not only agree on tasks, values, and visions, but you're also able to measure outcomes and reinforce issues that are important to you.

STAYING THE COURSE

-5-

You can have all your plans laid out in the most organized setup, but those plans won't mean squat if you don't stay on track amidst the hiccups, roadblocks, and endless distractions waiting for you when you look up from your calendar. You know this. I know this. We all know this, because we've all been there! Why then, are people still so easily swayed off course? And more importantly, how can you not be one of those people?

LIFE ACCORDING TO PLAN

LIFE ACCORDING TO LIFE

Here are five main reasons people get diverted from their goals:

Reason #1: They aren't truly committed to them.

That is, they love the idea of what it would be like once they've achieved their goal, but aren't so interested in the journey to get there. In fact, the very thought of having to get up at 5am, or practice for an hour every day for two years, or drive the extra 100 kilometres each week is enough for them to throw in the towel.

Think back to any of the goals you've been trying to achieve or have just set for yourself. If the process required to actually get there sounds a little something like this – ditch it. Stop right here. Don't go further. Not only are you unlikely to achieve this goal, but its very existence on your to-do list will drain your energy and bog down your self-image, because it will remind you of what you're not achieving (and don't truly plan to achieve). And you don't need that.

Reason #2: We're one tiny part of a huge system, and within that system lie endless uncontrollable, unpredictable events and factors.

This is true for almost everything, all the time. There's a difference between using this excuse as a cop-out – in which case please see reason #1 again – and being truly impacted by some event or news that infringes on your goal.

Reason #3: Impostor syndrome. Self-doubt. Blind spots. Losing sight of your goal.

Just as you get the ball rolling, that self doubt creeps in to cut you off: "who am I to_____?" or you've missed an important factor in what it means to achieve your goal, or you've lost confidence or momentum along the way.

Reason #4: Pings! Alerts! YouTube videos of cats. And babies. And hipsters making beer out of their breakfast cereal.

All the tech-based activities people engage in that begin as innocent check-ins and quickly spiral into hours of wasted time that could have otherwise been spent on their goals.

Reason #5: One word: BURNOUT.

It's pretty simple: you can't stay on track if you can't get out of bed.

So, these are my top five reasons. See any with your name on them? I know I've been guilty of all of these at one point or another. Thankfully, though, over the years I've come to discover tactics and tricks to help me outsmart, overcome, and avoid these threats to staying on track.

Laser Focus

I know that by now I've told you that THIS one thing is REALLY the thing you must do to get your life into deliberate, beautiful shape. And they're all true. But let me squeeze in one more (for now). If I owe my success and the success of my clients to one other trick, it's focus. And not just your typical understanding of focus, but the kind that my colleague Christian Marcolli refers to as laser focus: harnessing all of your energy and concentrating it on the one goal you're determined to achieve.

In other words, when working towards something deeply important to you that might be especially challenging, **you do *everything* and *anything* in your power and code of ethics to make it happen**. It's about feeling your hunger for something and being relentless and creative in the pursuit of its realization. Oftentimes, this will mean dropping everything else to a sub-optimal level for a short period of time, but just like a laser beam, your efforts will become exponentially powerful when you single-track your focus until the job is done.

Our family used laser focus when our middle son Tristan, now 18, was preparing to go to high school. He desperately wanted to get into a particular school that had a specialized five-year sports program. In order to get accepted, he would need to complete and pass a six-hour audition. As these things sometimes go, on the day of his audition he was rushed to the hospital for an emergency appendectomy. Great! Needless to say, he missed his audition. That's when the laser focus began.

At first, the staff were somewhat understanding and rescheduled his tryout. Unfortunately, in Tristan's recovery he had complications that led to 17 pounds of weight loss and anaemia. By the time he showed up for his audition he was so weak he didn't pass. He was devastated as he tried to explain himself, but the school told him it just wasn't meant to be. That's when our laser focus really kicked up into high gear.

I worked on this for 12 hours a day consciously and unconsciously for weeks. I bartered with a marketer I knew to work with Tristan on creative ways to get the school's acceptance. Together, all three of us worked on a sports CV, planned out a video about why he should get a second chance, explored community involvement to get media coverage if ever needed. I called the school nearly every day and networked with anyone we could who was connected to it. Robert and I even wrapped a Christmas gift for Tristan that said, "You got in!" and put it under the tree with the belief that it would help attract our vision.

I'll never forget receiving the message that he got in. I was in Latin America about to deliver a keynote. A few minutes before I went onstage I received the text from Robert and was so overjoyed that people in the crowd were excited for me! (Of course, I couldn't help but weave the story into my speech in broken Spanish, even though I barely know how to speak it!)

Tristan went on to absolutely love his high school and won two elite athletic awards of his five years there. The funny thing is that, to this day, none of us know exactly what it was that got him in. Was it the creative CV? The persistent calls? The volunteering? The hope and belief? Some combination? We still aren't sure which one landed, but that's why it was important for us to do everything in our power. If we had only called once we'd have better prayed to the high heavens that it would've been the thing that worked!

Laser focus is a mindset to adopt when facing acute, highly important goals like the one above – the kind that require your full attention. During these times, your Bin 2 values become Bin 3 values, because adaptation is required in order to achieve your number one vision without establishing unrealistic expectations for yourself and others. The best part about laser focus is that, once all is said and done, whether or not you were successful in achieving your goal, you will know that you left it all on the table with no regrets. And that's so much of what deliberate action is all about.

Brain Boxes

Our lives coexist and conflict. We work and parent. We travel for business and coach soccer practice. We have elderly parents who need care and children who need diaper changes, holiday events to attend and funerals to show up for. Sometimes, just when we feel on track with a goal in one area of our lives, another area unexpectedly demands our attention.

The concept I'm about to share is something I've been teaching clients for years but only adopted in this way when I began leading global virtual trainings through The Usheroff Institute. I loved the analogy that founder Roz Usheroff used and have been presenting it this way ever since. She coined the term "brain boxes," which is a tool that helps you manage life's opposing demands and stay focused on your main priority in the given moment.

Brain boxes work like this:

1. You're at home enjoying dinner with your family and hear your phone ring. You immediately feel anxious, as you know you missed a deadline today and it's more than likely that your boss is calling to chew you out. Instead of rushing away from the table, allow yourself to feel the anxiety for a minute and stay *with your family*.

2. Put that thought – that you need to check your call and deal with it – into a box in your brain labelled "work," and move it from the front of your brain to the back. Then, return to being mentally present with your family.

3. When the time comes, say 9pm when your kids have had their story and tuck-ins, pull the brain box back to the front of your brain and deal with business.

The reason for consciously compartmentalizing these emerging thoughts and responsibilities is so that you can effectively manage opposing worlds and the stresses that result. We could feel anxious all day long and never fully do the things that are right in front of us if we allowed ourselves to be swept up in the endless interruptions. The key is to think of your brain as having boxes in it that are prioritized from most important at the front to least important at the back. When the appropriate time comes for the given box, then deal with it!

Board of Directors

If you've been honest with your deepest values and greatest desires, chances are there are some pretty big goals on your list. It's likely that pursuing them will elicit a vast range of emotions over the course of your path towards their realization, from excitement and inspiration to hesitation and self-doubt.

Having people whom you trust and who believe in you can make a real difference when it comes to staying the course. This is your "village" or your "board of directors," as The Usheroff Institute puts it: the people from all corners of your life who care about you, support you, and see you as wholly capable. My own board of directors (BOD) has been the cornerstone of so much of the joy, success, and peace I have achieved over the years, both in my career and family life. They're my go-tos when I need help, advice, feedback, or words of encouragement, and my most devoted cheerleaders when it's time to celebrate successes.

Tarina's BOD

- Five close friends.
- Three close friends who are or were colleagues.
- My ex-professional mentor.
- My ex-boss.
- A colleague who is also an entrepreneur.

- My husband.
- My mom.
- My brother.
- My sister-in-law.
- My uncle.
- My aunt.
- One key customer.
- My three teenage kids.

When I'm in need of another's perspective, I select the members of my board that suit the context and reach out proactively and deliberately. And when I say reach out, I really mean I reach out. The titles of my emails read, "Urgent, action required – I need your help!" or "Action required – looking for candid feedback!" Then, usually within the next 24-hours or so (often 24-minutes, or 24-seconds), I receive their support. This support has been absolutely essential to me: my BOD is my reality check when in doubt, my eyes when I'm blind to something, and my most trusted advisers. Is their advice always what I want to hear? No! Is what they recommend what I always decide to do? Not necessarily. It's up to me what advice and feedback I choose to integrate into my actions. The key is that I know that I have a community of people who have my back. And just like everything else, this isn't about luck, this is about having deliberately devoted my life to building and sustaining each of these relationships.

How to Build Your Own BOD

1. Think of the people in your life who have already shown their loyalty to you, their faith in you, their candidness, and their honesty. Think of the people whom you trust, value, and admire, the people who challenge you and draw you out of your comfort zone. Consider people in both your professional and personal circles, people of different genders and values. Write a list of these names down.

2. Reach out and tell them why you'd love for them to be on your board, explaining your desire for their candidness and honesty. Then see what happens!

The other side of the coin is being on others' BOD. They may not request that you join their board in such a formal fashion, but you'll know when you're someone's go-to. My #1 motto is "relationships above all", and so the people who rely on me are my highest priorities and they know it. Just as I gain so much from my board, I also gain so much through being on the boards of others. Short of Google, your BOD may just be the best investment you could ever make.

Fiercely Managing Technology

If you don't already know my age, you will now. I was born in 1971 and the cell phone made its way into my generation's lives in 1995. I kept away from the smart phone craze while my kids were still little and finally gave in when the last one went to high school. Needless to say, I was at least five years behind everyone else. Looking back, I feel blessed to have lived so many years in a world where technology didn't take over my life the way it does today. Don't get me wrong – I adore technology. I'm attached to my iPhone, laptop, Apple TV, and all the ways these gadgets have simplified my life and saved me time. If I'm being honest with you, I feel as though I could no longer live well without my smartphone – I'm totally obsessed with the thing. And therein lies the problem....

All-too-often, our strongest beliefs, values, visions, and missions are buried and exchanged for the meaningless junk we find on our screens. Our precious attention has been compromised by the single ding of a text or email and hearing a notification has become more important than the person right in front of us. The really ironic thing? Most of the emails or texts we're getting aren't even that exciting! It's as though our brains think we've won some unexpected lottery, but no, it's usually something completely commonplace, or even spam! Despite the fact that technology can undoubtedly help us live deliberately in tremendous ways, when it's used without intention, it completely throws us off our game.

As a self-proclaimed recovering tech addict, here are some of the ways I deliberately manage technology:

Tarina's Ways of Fiercely Managing Technology

Personally:

- I don't sleep with my phone in my room unless airplane mode is on as an extra alarm when travelling for business.
- I "hide" my phone on myself from Friday night to Sunday evening at 7pm, religiously.
- On vacation, if I'm gone for one week I never check my email or texts (if I'm gone for two weeks I check and respond mid-vacation and then get back to relaxing).

As a couple:

- We always talk, cuddle and enjoy our mornings before checking our phones.
- We use a joint phone on weekends and only allow connection with my mom and kids and a few besties occasionally as a retreat (the same goes for when on vacation).
- Social media is managed with huge rules and alignment.

As a family:

- Up to 17-years-old, kids not allowed phones overnight in rooms.
- Up to 14-years-old, kids not allowed gadgets at cottage between 11:30am––6:00pm and didn't get them back unless they played outside for hours.
- On weekends, we lay on couches and chat, play games, or watch movies for periods of time without phones on us (I go around and crate the kids' phones while we're spending time together).
- We have zero tolerance for phones at dinner or when other adults are visiting for the holidays.

In her book *Thrive*, Arianna Huffington poses a question I encourage you to reflect on in your own use of technology: "To me, the key question is this: Does the technology deepen the experience, or does it diminish it?"

In what ways could you manage your technology better in order to protect your goals and visions? Strike up a conversation with your family and see what you come up with!

Rest. Relax. Refuel.

In the "Got Fuel?" chapter, we took a good look at all of the activities, responsibilities, and tasks in your life that either energize or drain you. When it comes to avoiding burnout, there's simply nothing more effective than upping those activities that allow for rest, relaxation, and refuelling, and diminishing as many sneaky energy drains as possible. For some, this can be really hard to do – especially those who need it the most!

It might take going through a series of burnouts before some people realize it's time for a change, but I'm thinking you're different. In order to stay on course, we simply must create space for leisure in our lives. We must play, nourish, nap, exercise, take a bath, read a book, make art, chat with friends, whatever. We must sometimes forget that we are bankers and lawyers, consultants and grocers, parents and children and, and, and! We need to habitually engage in the things that allow us to just be, as we are. We need to make time for being as wildly unproductive as possible, so that, when it's time to secure our work boots and change our kids' diapers, we can do so with gusto and vitality (maybe not the diapers).

Rest. Relax. Refuel. And do it with deliberateness!

MEASURING SUCCESS BY A BIKINI WAX (AND OTHER TACTICS)

-6-

"There's nothing like getting a beautiful bikini wax to help me unwind," said no one, ever.

Remember those packed lunches that help me evaluate the shifting of priorities in my life? Well, when it comes to measuring the success of my own work-life integration goals, I look to my perspective on bikini waxes for a clue. In short, if I've reached the point where I'm looking forward to having those 10 minutes to myself to lie down and "relax," I know I'm doing something wrong and need to course-correct.

Incorporating ways to regularly measure your success is essential to acting deliberately. For one, it allows you to catch any off-course trajectories early on in their journey, enabling you to lessen their consequences and even avoid hitting rock bottom in some cases. On the flipside, routinely assessing your level of success invites cause for celebration when things do go well. And if you're really committed to choosing and acting deliberately, there will be many little and big wins to celebrate.

So, how do you integrate measuring success into your own life?

Quarterly Bucket and Bin Reviews

Just as the name indicates, these reviews are to be done each quarter with reference to the buckets and bins in your life. You can do them once a season or at any other four points throughout the year. I find it easiest to establish specific months ahead of time so that they become ritualized. For example, I know that January, April, July, and October are my quarterly review months. It may not be the very same day within a given month each year, but I've set the expectation for myself and have it fixed in my calendar. Note: this is also when I do all of my frontloading, remember?

How to Do a Quarterly Bucket and Bin Review

1. Ensure you're in a space that you can relax and reflect in, then grab your notebook and a pen. Begin by drawing out the buckets in your life as they have been for the past few months. Where are your levels of satisfaction? How do they weigh up to where they were during your last review? Have circumstances changed since then that would explain any differences?

2. Then bring your bins to the table. Are your Bin 1 priorities reflected in the levels of your buckets? Have any of your Bin 1 priorities changed?

3. Where there is alignment, explore what you might be doing right to make it so. Where there is a gap, I encourage you to drill down and ask yourself why that might be the case. Then, brainstorm ways you can create more harmony between your buckets and bin items.

This exercise is a process of reflection and evaluation, followed by tweaking. Once you've thoughtfully considered your current buckets of life and Bin 1, 2, and 3 priorities, you should be able to clearly pinpoint what's going right and what might require some attention. Of course, as circumstances and priorities change, so will all of these factors. The key takeaway is to identify your current values and establish whether or not they're showing up in the buckets of your life. Acquiring this knowledge will enable you to revamp your strategies as required and keep you heading towards your North Star.

In some cases you'll find that the gap between your buckets and bins requires the collaboration of someone else, in which case it's important to get that person on-board and bought into your vision.

My clients also use this strategy when it comes to assessing how well their kids are doing. As their children grow older, they might do this with their partners or by themselves once a year instead of every quarter. The process itself also slightly differs, in that the labels of buckets are tweaked for their kids and include academic, social, emotional, sibling relationships if applicable, relationships with parents, health, etc. They may compare how their Bin 1 priorities relate to their kids' buckets in their eyes, but this is a secondary consideration. The main outcome from this review is to figure out which areas each child is doing well in, and which areas require more attention. For example, if one child is struggling in school they may realize that they need to hire a tutor, or if another child is having a hard time socially, perhaps they'll increase their family time with cousins to balance the scales. Reviewing your own kids' buckets is a great way to be deliberate in your parenting as much as the other areas of your life.

Celebrate Success and Never Give Up

When you make deliberate choices and act accordingly, you can expect there to be several causes for celebration in your life. I'm a firm believer that each day should hold little treats to keep you encouraged, in addition to the substantial celebrations across your accomplishments. These treats have become rituals for me, like wearing a high-quality lip-gloss or ordering books online, and serve to remind me of my progress and motivate me to keep pressing ahead. After all, isn't one of the main reasons you're choosing to live deliberately to increase the amount of joy and gratitude you experience?

The beauty of life is that, each day, we can create moments of joy if we so choose. I've made it my commitment to have something to look forward to every day – so much so that no day is ever worth eating a banana.

Allow me to explain.

When I was young I discovered that I was allergic to bananas. It wasn't a severe allergy, but it was bad enough to leave me feeling sick and out of commission for the day. I've been wanting to get a test to see if I'm still allergic to bananas, since I would love to enjoy them in my smoothies and all kinds of breakfasts and desserts. The problem is: no day is worth potentially ruining! I've created a life that includes something to look forward to each day, no matter how small that might be, and so the thought of willingly putting my day at risk of being a write-off is simply out of the question! This is something I never take for granted, either. Instead, I count my blessings all the time and work to create and re-create a beautiful life every day.

How to Celebrate Your Successes

1. Have a look at your calendar and establish which months are best for you to hold your own quarterly bucket and bin reviews. If you have a partner and/or children, consider organizing multiple reviews.

2. Think of the small and big ways you can celebrate successes along the way. Write a list and then, when you've accomplished something as small as putting your phone away during dinner or as large as reaching a milestone on one of your visions, refer to your list and see which method of treat or celebration suits the occasion.

REMINDERS, MANTRAS, & THINGS TO KNOW:

You are what you do.
Do wisely, over and over (and over) again.

Work back from your ideal state to find
your starting point. Then go.

Your people need your love in action.

Where there's a plan, there's a way.

Keep calm and laser-focus, brain box it, BOD it,
manage technology, and REST.

Don't wait until you're looking forward to a bikini
wax
to do your quarterly review.

Celebrate the little wins as well as the big ones.

BECOME WHAT MATTERS

SUSTAINING, PROTECTING, AND EVER-EVOLVING YOUR DELIBERATE LIFE

"My mission in life is not merely to survive, but to thrive; and to do so with some passion, some compassion, some humour, and some style."

– Maya Angelou

YOU'RE NOT REALLY ONE IN A MILLION

- 1 -

I'll bet that at some point in your life you did something so great, so different, so totally you that someone noticed and said, "Wow! You know, you're really one in a million!" In other words: what you just did was totally unique, and it surprised and delighted me. But the truth is, you're not really one in a million at all. According to today's Google search, you're approximately one in 7.046 billion – that's how truly unique you are! That's how *truly* special you are! The question, now, is this:

Do you know the ways in which you are unique and special?

Do you know what makes you truly remarkable?

Becoming what matters stems from a deep sense of knowing yourself. Part of knowing yourself is informed by your values, priorities, and actions, but this is only a piece of the puzzle – a big piece at that – but there's more to it. Have you ever met someone so outrageously themselves that the only way to describe them is "radiant"? We might assume that this person has been choosing and acting what matters for some time, but there's something else going on. There's an inexplicable sense of freedom and peace in the way this person moves through the world, and you can't help but want to be closer to it. You're left affected after, wondering what it would be like to experience life that way, to be so wholeheartedly and unapologetically yourself. This last part, being unreservedly you, is part of what it means to become what matters. And I say become, because there's never an arrival so long as we're living and breathing, but instead it's a continual process of becoming, of digging deeper, of sustaining what is true and of evolving and expanding the rest.

In 2003, marketing and leadership guru Seth Godin released a book called *Purple Cow: Transform Your Business by Being Remarkable*. The book was a huge success, as was Seth's TED Talk on it. The gist of it is this: with so much out there, in order to really stand out – to be remarkable – we must do something worthy of remark, something as worthy of remark as a purple cow on the side of the road. The context of this was advertising, but the concept applies to you and to me just the same. After all, just like businesses, we have a brand. You may not even be aware of it, but the fact is that, when people think of us, certain expectations and impressions come to mind. Roz Usheroff explains this concept in her executive presence trainings and claims that your brand is not what you think of yourself but what others think of you.

What we become known for defines us to others, and whether or not we're explicitly aware of our brand, we typically end up internalizing these impressions simply by the way we're treated. And so the cycle goes. This tendency to internalize other's impressions of us makes understanding what makes us remarkable all the more important. The more aware you are of your unique packaging of gifts, talents, and traits, the more positive and deliberate an impact you can have on your brand. I want to make something clear here: being remarkable is not necessarily being the best or the first at something. I say this because when I work on this concept in trainings and coaching sessions, some will say to me, "But Tarina there will always be someone better at _____ than I am, no matter how great I am at it!" or "Tarina, it's already been said/done before." These statements are absolutely true, but they also don't matter. Having a remarkable brand is about being worthy of remark, and being worthy of remark is not simply about being great at something or the first to do it, but about being both great and *unique in your approach*. How can you do that? By focusing on your strengths and continuously developing them, and by bringing your entirely individual flare to your craft, which will come naturally so long as you give yourself permission to do so. Remember, you're not one in a million, you're one in 7.046 billion. There is no way that you cannot be remarkably you if you allow it.

Some of us spend so much of our lives focusing on everything outside of ourselves that we haven't taken the time to really identify what our gifts are in the first place. Whether or not you've already done some digging in this area, coming to know yourself and building your remarkable brand is an ongoing process.

How do you do it? Here are a few great ways:

How to Discover What Makes You Remarkable

1. Speak with your trusted BOD. Ask each of them what they think it is that shines inside of you, that you have a special flare for, or that they love and admire about you.

2. Take note of what people ask you for help with. If someone is consistently coming to you for advice on something or for a helping hand, acknowledge it to yourself and consider asking them what they think makes you the right person to reach out to.

3. Take note of compliments you receive. Again, is there a pattern here? This is all valuable feedback that you can harness and expand upon to create greater impact in your life. Identifying what is remarkable about you is part of leading a deliberate life. What others appreciate about you is key.

4. Ask for feedback from people whom you respect. They don't have to be in your BOD, but if you feel they know you well enough to understand your character and have

seen you in action, ask if they'd be open to sharing their thoughts with you.

5. Sit down and write out all of the things you loved to do as a child. What came naturally to you? What did you get lost in? Do any of the skills or qualities exercised back then still come easily to you now?

You came into this world with all the fixings to be nobody but yourself. And nobody can be you as well as you can. It's your job to figure out your gifts and – most importantly – your own special way of going about them, because once you do, you won't be able to be anything but remarkable.

WGAF(F)

Before you go any further, I'd like to (respectfully) ask you something: **Who gives a f*ck?** What I mean is:

- You can read this book, but if you don't start making deliberate choices, then *WGAF*?
- You can make deliberate choices, but if you don't start taking deliberate action, then *WGAF*?
- You can take deliberate actions, but if you don't continue to pursue deliberate growth, then *WGAF*?
- And, when you do all these things but play small, then, really – *WGAF*?

What's it all for?

Imagine if Thomas Edison lived deliberately but played small. We'd all be sitting in the dark, wouldn't we? There'd be an electric light bulb stashed away somewhere while we'd continue huddling around a flame. It'd be tragic!

Far too many people hold the belief that they shouldn't reveal their remarkable selves and gifts to others. But I say: **if your value**

isn't visible, how can you truly be all that you are? How can you truly be of service to others? I call this the Who Gives a F*ck Factor (WGAFF): you can stretch and grow and encompass all kinds of amazing qualities and create all kinds of amazing things, but if nobody knows this, then they cannot be fully expressed or actualized.

As you continue to make deliberate choices, take deliberate actions, and become what matters to you, know that you must bring your value to visibility if you care to have a greater impact in the world. Nobody will know the person they have in their circle if you hide your remarkable self. Most importantly, perhaps the only way you'll ever truly become what matters to you is by allowing yourself to shine, as you were meant to all along.

HEAD AND HEART

-2-

One characteristic that extraordinary people share is their mastery of working with their heads and hearts in tandem. In decades past, leaders were seen as those who made decisions and took action entirely from a place of logic. But when we actually reflect on some of the world's most influential change-makers (think people like Martin Luther King Jr. and Oprah Winfrey), it's clear to see that using both their heads and their hearts – and accessing those of others – was the most powerful way to create an impact.

To become what truly matters to you, it's not enough to lead solely with your head or your heart. Instead, you need to find a balance between reason and intuition, logic and emotion. My colleague, Christian Marcolli, coined this perfectly during our leadership trainings as "leading with your head and heart", and I've come to see how doing so is important in most contexts. Think about how this applies in your own life: do you lead more with your head or your heart? Chances are, you're more comfortable accessing one over the other. And that's largely because of the way you're wired and the environment you were raised in. The good news is that either area can always be developed and improved; it's never too late.

I learned how to truly incorporate my heart into the picture later on in life thanks to my BFF, Vanessa. It's funny to think that it wasn't until I was in my early forties that I really understood what incorporating my heart meant. Despite being a "people person," for the better part of my life, I relied on my strategic mind to pave the path. Using my head certainly served me in many ways, but there was always something deep within me that felt as though I was still chasing *something*. Through Vanessa's teachings on how to be unapologetically vulnerable with her, I learned how to extend this way of being with others in my life. With this, I found myself accessing the heart that had been knocking at my door for years. Being shown the way by my friend, learning what it was to truly be in touch with my emotions no matter how painful, to be authentic no matter how frightening, was the key to the freedom I had been chasing deep inside. And geez! Accessing this part of myself and bringing my heart to the table is so much more effective than only leading with my head. No more wasting time with endless small talk, or taking ages to develop trusting relationships with clients and friends. Using my head and heart in synchronicity has enabled me to connect with others more deeply and use my head more intelligently. It has allowed me to better understand the needs of others and deliver more meaningful work. The same goes for the other way around.

No matter how emotionally intelligent or compassionate you are, if you're unable to bring your head to the party you'll find yourself standing in the sidelines while the others get on with making the difference. In order to truly succeed, to become what matters to you, you will need to nurture and exercise both your head and your heart.

The purpose of this chapter is merely to get you thinking about where you currently stand on the head-to-heart scale. While the learnings in this book will help you develop both your head and heart faculties, I encourage you to get curious and explore them more deeply through other resources. Some of my favorites include self-help books, therapy, trainings, and conversations with those whom I consider to be masters of their head and heart.

DON'T LET GREAT BE THE ENEMY OF GOOD

-3-

I want you to try a social experiment. Ask the next person you speak with – it can be anyone at all – how they're doing. Chances are the conversation will unfold a little something like this:

You: "Hi! How are you?"

Them: "Ugh, so busy!"

You: "How was your weekend?"

Them: "Good, but too busy!"

You: "How was your vacation?"

Them: "So busy that we need a vacation from our vacation!"

It doesn't matter if you're speaking with a CEO or a part-time student, most often their answer will be some version of "too busy!" Isn't that a problem? I wish these conversations sounded more like this:

You: "Hi! How are you?"

Them: "Great! A lot on my plate lately but I've prioritized my work and feel good about it."

You: "How was your weekend?"

Them: "Amazing! I got so much done at home, relaxed a lot, and feel like I'm living in my own sanctuary now."

You: "How was your vacation?"

Them: "Awesome! I made relaxation my 'number one', didn't answer a single email and completely disconnected!"

Doesn't that sound better?

Somewhere along the way, society adopted the idea that "busyness" should be worn as a badge of honor. In other words, we've come to equate being busy with being important and pride ourselves on the stack of our demands. Here's the bad news: you may feel important if you're busy, but the two certainly aren't synonymous. In fact, when I hear someone continuously profess how busy they are I can't help but think, "Oh my, you must be so inefficient!" This busyness sham is quite truly the opposite of deliberate living and becoming what matters to you.

Getting stuck in a Busyness as Badge (BAB) mentality stems from the fact that, when we prioritize one thing, by default we de-prioritize something else. People with a BAB mentality fear what their lives might look like, how they will be regarded, or how they will see themselves if they sacrifice some things for the sake of others, and so they continue trying to be great at everything. The result? Just look at the two types of conversations above. Which would you prefer to have?

The other side of the BAB coin is complete inactivity. For some, being confronted with the reality that they can't sustain a do-it-all approach drives them to do nothing at all. And so, we have two extremes: people who don't accept that they can't do it all and drive themselves into the ground trying and people who do accept that they can't do it all but don't even bother doing something.

Let's have a look at this through an example:

Your friend sends you a text about her failing love life just as you're running into a meeting. You promised your son that, right after your meeting, you would pick him up from school and go for lunch together. Following that, you have more meetings and then are joining your husband after work for a parent-teacher interview. Despite caring about your friend and her feelings, on this day filled with your Bin 1s (values related to your immediate family and career), your friend's text is simply not as important. In reality, you have three options:

a. Ignore the text and write back another time when you have more time.

b. Fire off a quick, "Sounds tough! Crazy day here but want to hear *all*. Will call tomorrow! Big hugs."

c. Cancel lunch with your son and call your friend. After all, she needs you.

After discussing these concepts in trainings around the globe, I've come to find that when it comes down to it, most people will either go for option a or c. However, when we look at option b, it's plain to see that this is the one that will honor your highest priorities while still maintaining your friendship (so long as you do write back another day).

In between the spectrum of doing everything and doing nothing lies the sweet spot. This is the place where your Bins 1, 2, and 3 are upheld in proportion to their position, the place where your effort is a direct reflection of your priorities. People who live from this sweet spot are those who understand the concept of not letting great be the enemy of good, or my 70/150% rule.

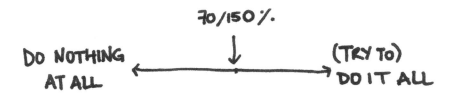

The 70/150% Rule

This rule is simple: in order to become what matters to you, some things will demand your very best (150%), while others will merely require your "good enough" (70%). The values that are at the top of your priority list – your Bin 1 items – are given 150% of your devotion and effort, whereas everything else receives your 70%. The beautiful thing about this rule is that by giving your all to your highest priorities, you will become truly important in the areas that matter most to you. And when it comes to providing 70% of yourself to the rest? Nobody usually cares, or notices, hence "good enough"! Note that I don't aim for 100% with everything, because, if we try to give our 100% to everything, we are sure to run out of fuel. As I said in the "Got Fuel?" chapter, part of being deliberate is treating our efforts with a sprint-recover approach: sprint (100-150%), recover (0-70%), sprint (100-150%), recover (0-70%).

Here are a few examples of my own 70/150%ers:

(Some of) Tarina's 70/150% Items

70% Good Enough	150% Great
Send clients Christmas gifts in January when quieter and our family Christmas card out on Valentine's Day.	Be totally present and engaged when I am presenting, delivering, coaching, tucking my children in or eating dinner with my family.
Host 25-person parties but ask everyone to bring most of the food, use plastic dishes, and have guests help clean up too.	When someone I love is ill or not well, I offer them all the care, attention, support, and research needed to get them back on track.
Show up for meetings but multitask on the telecons where I'm not a major participant and do my grocery list when the topic's not relevant to me.	Watch *This is Us* TV show anytime, anywhere.

Life will never stop demanding it all from us, but if we use the 70/150% rule, we can make sure that we're the ones in the driver's seat.

What does your 70/150% list look like?

LET GO, BE FREE

- 4 -

When we practice deliberate living and have a set destination in mind, even with the best of tools, tips, and tricks, life doesn't always unfold the way we'd like it to.

Part of becoming what matters is truly letting go of the hope that you can control the people and circumstances around you. How does this sit with control freaks like me? It's a tough one! This being said, mastering the art of letting go is vital in birthing our dreams and visions into reality, as it reconnects us to what is within our own span of control. While we can massively and deliberately influence others, we can't control them.

Suitcases and Umbrellas

I received some incredible advice on the subject a number of years ago from my Aunt, Terri Harrison, also the VP of consulting and senior strategist at TAP Strategy and HR Consulting, mother, and general expert in many things family-related. At the time that I reached out to her, my son Nicholas was entering high school. What you first need to know is that Nicholas is our eldest. He's the one who made us parents, who turned us from "individual contributors" as the business world puts it, into leaders. And in all honesty, he's the one who made us deliberate. When he was born, it was the first time we decided to really examine our values and how we did things. It was also the first time we became responsible for the wellbeing of someone else. So when Nicholas' group of best friends since kindergarten began breaking up as they moved to high school, we tried to protect him as we always had. And when I say protect, I mean I got into full "mama bear mode": I constantly worried, lost sleep, tried to get the parents involved, sought therapy for my concerns, and strategized a plan to get his social life on track. The thing was, they were my plans and not his. What I didn't realize at the time was that it was no longer my job to be so involved in our son's life anymore. Just like when Nicholas was born, it was instead time for Robert and me to evaluate our beliefs and boundaries so that they would reflect our change in circumstances: our son was becoming a teenager.

This was really hard.

How much should we include ourselves in his relationships with friends?

His choices?

His emotional world?

It was a new stage for us as a family, and sometimes I felt as though my heart would break in two from the heaviness of it all. This is when my Aunt Terri explained her theory of Suitcases and Umbrellas: when we start off as parents with small children and as leaders with direct reports, our role is to assist and protect, i.e. to help carry the heavy suitcases of others and hold umbrellas over their heads when it rains. With their loads on our shoulders, we juggle tons of suitcases and umbrellas to make sure their arms don't get tired and their heads don't get wet. In the process, we tend to get soaked and exhausted. But slowly, in time and with intention, we must give over those suitcases and teach them how to hold their own umbrellas. At first, we watch helplessly as their suitcases drag on the ground and they forget to take their umbrellas with them, but we watch from afar anyways as they find their own approaches. We must let go of control and equip them with responsibilities that will enable them to become independent and autonomous, while also lightening our own loads in the process. And eventually, in some cases, they will come to carry ours.

With the advice of my Aunt Terri and through clenched teeth, we let go of the reins and let Nicholas deal with this change the way he knew how to. And you know what? When we finally stepped back, we saw him handle the situation in his own beautiful way. We witnessed him create new friendships and find happiness and strength in the process. Years later, we see how this experience served Nicholas in the long run through his attitude and his resilience. The process was hard but we needed to trust it and our son – we needed to hold him as the wholly capable person he is.

We are not meant to take on the full loads of others and sustain them. As parents and leaders, we are meant to set others free. And with their freedom come their own choices and ways of doing things that are beyond our control. The goal is that the initial help and guidance provided to them as we carried their suitcases and umbrellas (as well as our own!) is enough for them to now build a solid foundation upon which they can shape their lives and careers. Our role is to trust the process and the people, to hold each of them as wholly capable, and to treat them in this way.

Analogies simplify things, but in all honesty, this was a long and tiring process. I now try to help people find a much shorter path than I myself took and make it my life's work to help people live deliberate lives in ways that were not known or accessible to me at the time. One of the most transformational ways to put suitcases and umbrellas into action is through delegation.

Delegation

Delegation is the art and science of accomplishing work through others, and one of my favorite ways to let go of control and bring my most important priorities to life.

You simply can't take on everything yourself if you want to save your energy for your Bin 1 values. By delegating, you're able to free up time for higher-level tasks, reduce your stress, and enhance your value by practicing your credibility as a parent and leader. It also gives others the opportunity to practice their own skillsets, up their self-esteem and build their potential. Sounds great, right? Here's how to go about it:

How to Become a Delegation Master (at Work and at Home)

1. Delegate an entire project instead of one task as much as possible and be clear about why it needs to be done. This clarity will help motivate the person and lend to a sense of accomplishment once the project is completed.

2. Choose the right person for the job: pick those whose judgment and competence you trust, or develop trust in others by giving them structured assignments with ample support. When it comes to delegating at home, find the right projects to match the areas you believe are important for your child or team to develop and build confidence.

3. Be specific about what a great result looks like.

4. Provide a deadline and a timeframe for milestones.

5. Be accessible and offer help when required. Focus on coming up with solutions through collaboration.

6. Finally, and perhaps most importantly, offer feedback and support throughout the process. Everyone needs encouragement and the feeling of being valuable.

Tarina's Delegation List

Home:

- When my daughter was little and liked making beds, one of her chores was making ours too.

- The kids make our meals once a week.

- My son, Tristan, does our laundry.

- All household tasks at the cottage and at home are shared between the five of us.

- Emma does all the Christmas wrapping.

- Each week, I think of tasks that Robert can do to help and we discuss them on Tuesday List Day.

- I hire help whenever I can afford it: if my work and salary increases, so does my paid help.

- We order our groceries online and have them delivered.

- When planning events and parties, I give everyone a task.

- If I'm researching something and don't have time to read all of the articles I want, I hire each of my kids to read one of them and summarize the main points for me.

- I have my kids figure out their own consequences if they've done something that justifies it (usually they're worse than what I would come up with!).

Work:

In many ways, delegation is simplification. I try to simplify any process or project by 30% and totally get rid of another 25%. I'll likely delegate another 25%, leaving me with 20% of it to focus on in a more strategic way.

- Anything I am not good at I look to my team – look to who is best at it – and delegate it immediately.
- I delegate anything administrative or operational.
- If I don't have direct reports, I find colleagues to barter services with.
- I get really curious and ask colleagues what they love to do in life and ask for help in that area when I need it.

Think about your own suitcases and umbrellas:

How heavy is your load?

How much are you juggling?

Where do you need to let go?

What can you begin to delegate more of today?

PLAY BY YOUR OWN RULES

- 5 -

I was on a plane recently and, as always, used my time in the air to get work done. Somewhere between Montreal and New York, I pulled out my notepad and began writing what would become my author's note. Towards the end of the trip, the man next to me leaned over and asked if I was a writer. "How did you know?" I replied. He said, "Because I saw the way you were writing – it was ferocious! Let me guess what your book is about: it's about playing by your own rules." Though I hadn't thought of it in those exact terms, I was amazed at how well he called it. Had he been reading over my shoulder? How could he know? I asked him and he told me that he had been observing me in the lounge of the airport and was struck by how I handled myself.

As you can probably imagine, I always come to the airport prepared. Despite my dread of packing, I do so with great care and, whenever possible, only travel with a carry-on to keep my travels as simplified and quick as possible. On this trip, while waiting in the lounge area before boarding, an announcement blared out of the loudspeaker notifying everyone that the plane was at full capacity and some carry-ons would need to be checked. Of course, no one volunteered. Like me, it's likely that many others had brought carry-ons to speed their own travel times. A minute later, a flight attendant approached me and said that my bag looked a little large, so she was going to ask me to check it. I politely but assertively said, "I'm sorry, I travel all the time and am sure that my bag is the legal carry-on size. I will be in a hurry when I get to New York and brought a carry-on for this purpose. If ever my bag doesn't fit, then I will be happy to check it, but I don't believe that will be the case." She said ok and moved on to the next person!

The man sitting with me on the flight said he heard how I spoke with the attendant and admired what I did. When I asked why he wouldn't have done the same, he said he'd be too afraid – that he would feel badly about refusing her request. "Were her needs more important than yours?" I asked. "The truth is, some people will never stand up for what they want, and they won't get what they need as a result. **If you want to live a life where your priorities come to fruition, you'll need to care a whole lot less about what other people think of you.** In fact, you really will need to play by your own rules!"

Becoming what matters is a well-earned position to grow into and only comes after continuous, deliberate choice-making and action-taking. After all of your efforts, are you going to give up your priorities over what people think of you? Those priorities and needs are yours – own them! Of course, there is tremendous value in receiving the feedback of others whom we value and trust. They help us understand who we are and where we are going. This said, we must always evaluate that feedback before integrating it into our lives so that we're not ruled by the opinions of others. Speaking your truth and asserting your needs is simply the only way you can fully live into the best vision you have of and for yourself. To preserve this vision – and your sanity for that matter – you need to create a set of your own rules to play by. So long as they are formed from a place of integrity, are born of good intentions, and don't conflict with the wellbeing of others or the law, go for them! Doing so will cut out a layer of complexity in your life, will help you avoid rumination, and will generally make your experiences a whole lot more enjoyable.

One of my client's favorite examples of how I play by my own rules is what my family refers to as "May Day". In our home, everyone's birthday falls around the same time: mine on October 9th, Emma's December 6th, Robert's January 17th, Tristan's February 4th, and worse off is my eldest son Nicholas – December 31st, aka New Year's Eve. After the flurry of my birthday, Thanksgiving, Emma's birthday and Christmas, everyone is totally done with gifts and is caught up in the hype of ringing in the New Year instead. We tried making his birthday a stand-out success for many years until it dawned on me that we could take matters into our own hands. And so, May Day was born.

May Day occurs towards the end of May each year and is Nicholas' postponed, "proper" birthday celebration. While we still mark his actual birthday on the day, all gifts and parties are held in May on a day that everyone can get together. This way, Nicholas gets to have his special day when everyone is happy to celebrate it! It also provides another reason to get the family together when our kids move out of the house. Everyone will be together for Christmas already, so by putting his birthday in the quieter month of May, I can ensure there is another point throughout the year when we'll gather.

Here are some of my other favorite self-made rules to live by:

Tarina's Play by the Rules of my Own Game

- I like sleeping in on vacation so if check out is 11:00am and breakfast is until 10:00am I always manage to negotiate breakfast for 11:30 am and checkout at 2:00pm (no extra charge).
- When I entertain, everyone brings a prepared dish and leaves with their dirty dish (unless they clean it themselves).
- When I have local guests at the cottage, I tell them that if they want fresh sheets to bring them (non-local guests get fresh sheets and a made up bed).

- At the airport on business trips, I show up late and then they put me first in line at security.
- I never accept a "no" if I really want something – I'm kind but assertive.
- I always demand good service.
- When my kids were little, on New Year's Eve I used to put the clock ahead by two hours to get them in bed by 10:00pm.
- I never pick up something I can have delivered.
- I never do something I can easily delegate.
- I only make the quality of packed lunch I feel capable of at that stage of my life.

Clearly, being a conformist or domestic is not in my Bin 1! Many of my rules – and believe me I have a whole lot more – are time savers, and saving time equals having more time to put towards my Bin 1 and visions.

What rules have you already created for yourself?

What new rules can you make to help you protect your visions?

LIVING LIFE AS A SPONGE

-6-

What do the best of the best do to become that way? Seeking the answer to this question over and over again has made me a better entrepreneur, parent, partner, and friend. The reality is that there are always smarter, more experienced, and more evolved people out there than you and me. And thank goodness for that, because we get to use their wisdom and advice to better our own lives, if we so choose. This mentality is the premise of my mantra, one I learned from my mom: **get curious**. Soak up all the good stuff from the greatest. Live life as a sponge.

Any expert will tell you, becoming and sustaining your best is no accident. It's the result of continuous learning and skill building, of openness, humility and, as writer Elizabeth Gilbert puts it, of "following your curiosity". The very fact that you're holding this book in your hands and reading these words is a testament to your own curiosity, openness, and sponge-like mentality, and I honor you for it! Doing so helps us avoid mistakes made by others who've been there before us and provides us with unique perspectives on approaches we might've never considered otherwise.

One of my favorite ways to express my curiosity is directly with others. Asking people *extremely specifically* how they do what they do, or how they've achieved what they have, is not only beneficial to you, but also rewarding for them. When you ask thoughtful questions with sincere interest it allows you to get right to the core of what you're after without getting lost in small talk. Deeper connections are made and the opportunity for two-way learning arises.

My own approach to living life as a sponge is as deliberate as everything else. When I know someone is the best at something or, if I admire someone, I will seek that person out and request a meeting. I aim to have lunch with successful entrepreneurs at least three times a month to both keep my own learning momentum going and to network. As for the home front, I once invited Vanessa over to teach me how to be emotionally intelligent and vulnerable (as I mentioned in the "Head and Heart" chapter). We spent three hours in my living room: her teaching, me taking notes and re-reading them to her to ensure I got it all right. Another time, I did the same with Leah, who is a master of travelling with her kids. Once before a big trip with the whole family, I called Leah and asked her to describe *exactly* what she did when travelling with young ones: how to deal with jetlag, how to survive the long flights, how to keep each kid entertained, you name it. And, step-by-step, she spelled it out for me and really helped me turn those travels from anticipated chaos to as good as it gets with three kids stuck in the air for several hours!

I'm also constantly reaching out to my BOD for guidance and wisdom. No matter what stage of life you're at, I encourage you to look around, think of those you admire and get in touch with them. Chances are, people will be extremely flattered and generous with their time and wisdom.

SPONGE LIFE

SOAKIN' UP THAT WISDOM

Ever been envious of someone? Ever admired someone? Living the sponge life challenges us to raise the bar for the quality of our own lives. It uses those feelings of contrast, of wanting something we don't yet have, whether through envy or admiration, and turns them from a state of lack or aspiration to a state of possibility and inspiration. As you engage in the sponge life and apply all of your learnings into daily practices, not only will you notice changes unfolding but others will, too. People will begin to regard you as someone they admire and will come-a-knockin' on your door to hear how you've done it. Becoming what matters is palpable. It's what everyone wants and what everyone has the fundamental right to pursue. And it all begins with curiosity.

KINTSUKUROI

-7-

For me, 2014 was a sort of teardown-rebuild time. Actually, it was more like a demolition-rebuild. Much of what I knew to be "my life" was blown apart, and I was left facing a new landscape I hadn't anticipated. I realized that this next chapter presented me with some critical choices: bury my head in the sand, accept what was and settle, or accept what was and find a way back to the kind of contentment I had known before. It took weeks to come to terms with my reality, as well as a decision point, but "beautiful above all" became the mantra that would eventually lead me to the fulfilment I had longed for.

There is a saying that goes, "The true life of the bowl…began the moment it was dropped." It refers to Kintsukuroi, a Japanese art form in which the cracks of broken ceramics are repaired with a mix of gold and resin. In doing so, these fractures are transformed from flaw to feature, the piece from a sense of brokenness to a symbol of resilience and the beauty in imperfection. By being dropped and broken open, the bowl's vulnerabilities are revealed and through its repair with gold, a new sense of uniqueness and vitality is born.

All of us have cracked bowls.

Each and every one of us.

And each and every one of us has the choice to repair with gold, to make it "beautiful above all". To run our fingers over the cracks, to pick up the broken pieces and to realize that what we hold in our hands is opportunity. It is the chance to look at our bowl – our life – with a new perspective, perhaps for the first time.

The message of Kintsukuroi gives me tremendous comfort and power, knowing that so long as we are alive it is never too late to honor and make beautiful this one life we have, regardless of how perfectly imperfect it may be. To know that with each day comes a new chance to meet our lives with our highest values and visions.

Your life may be a cracked bowl, but you are the repairer. The deliberate effect is the gold woven throughout your life, the beauty placed within the cracks, and the remarkable way it all fits together. It is the charm, the integrity, and the power you feel as you craft your one masterpiece called, "Your Life".

Go create something absolutely beautiful.

REMINDERS, MANTRAS, & THINGS TO KNOW:

Be you – the world needs you.

WGAFF

Use your head AND your heart.

Remember the 70/150% rule.

When the time is right,
let go of those suitcases and umbrellas.

Honor your priorities and play by your own rules.

The sponge life = the way forward.
Follow your curiosity.

Repair with gold. It is in you.

AFTERWORD

Tarina is by far the most deliberate human being I know. So deliberate, in fact, that it drove me a little insane at times – that is, until I understood the true power of it. "What's wrong with trusting the process?" I asked. "Let the universe decide," I would offer. But there is none of that for Tarina. She is full of plans and purpose, and her deliberateness is unmatched and unwavering. Against all odds, I have seen her triumph personally and professionally in situations where her belief and actions were simply unrealistic, and yet she won out.

The interesting thing about admiring Tarina's ways was that when I tried her approach for myself, I realized that it could also work for me. Once I saw the proof in my own life, I was totally converted. It's simple: being deliberate really matters. I have even come to the conclusion that it may actually be the only thing that matters when we are looking to achieve a goal or find success in our lives, regardless of what that success may look like.

When Tarina and I worked together in pharmaceuticals, she came across news that there was a global award to be won in our field of HR. Without hesitation she marched into my office and said, "Let's win Canada an award – let's do this!" Before I could say otherwise, she was off working on her plans day after day, (on top of her regular role leading organizational development), and we won! Working on her plan together, we created an impactful program that served our employees and was so outstanding it beat out all others across the world. In the development process, if anyone had doubts or a lack of confidence, Tarina was there to put everyone back on track and lead the way towards our vision and goal. In her mind it was crystal clear: with laser-focus we were winning, and we did.

This powerful woman changed me in many ways as a person, too. The learning started in a very unusual way for me. The private person that I am, I tended to deal with my personal concerns in my head, letting in only my very closest people and even then I preferred to solve in solitude. So, the story starts back in 2010 when I was struggling with my then seven-year-old daughter who was finding no friends, making school a challenge and leaving a heaviness in my heart. Tarina noticed my burden and encouraged me to talk – a courageous and bold move on her side, given I was her boss and most definitely not a talker. She smartly accessed my issue in a business fashion with flip charts, pens, and brainstorming. After a while, we decided that her daughter would befriend mine, and that we would bring the two together. I was not convinced about this; forcing kids together never worked. However this was different, Tarina was deliberate in her approach and went about the meet-up with strategic intent. She briefed her daughter on the mission and set out the challenges and expectations. She never demanded friendship but was clear that empathy and kindness would be enough.

Our daughters met about four times in the following three years, always short but with both parties willing. Nearly nine years later, this relationship is still very meaningful to them both. It's hard to describe what happened, but in our moments of darkness when my daughter needed a friend, she found Emma who showed her kindness. Tarina was deliberate about her approach and her involvement – never demanding, always focused. The impact was simply staggering.

I have since adopted this approach both at work and at home and now know everything is possible. I now consider my desires that once seemed impossible to be within my scope and reach. You just have to want it hard enough and rigorously prioritize – it's about what you say yes to and what you say no to. It's about minimizing the noise in your life to get to the gold of what matters to you. It's about what you really want to become and becoming it. This approach is hard work, while also being surprisingly easy. The hard work is in your own head, but Tarina will be there to help you get past that. A word of warning, however: this approach takes vulnerability and honest self-reflection. It is in this area that Tarina will role model and be your most remarkable guide. I have never met anyone quite so willing to tell her story, quite so open to feedback, and quite so dedicated to making a difference in the lives of others.

This approach has changed me.

Tarina has changed me.

She has shown me that other ways are possible and that only through daring can you grow and help those you love the most – and that includes yourself. The teachings of Tarina go deep and yet are remarkably simple. She is my teacher, a wise colleague, and someone I will always cherish. She has become a safe haven for so many around the world wanting to learn from her and her wise and impactful strategies. With playfulness, brilliance, and heart, this girl delivers.

Lean in and be inspired, it's worth a try. Once you do, you'll realize that being deliberate is the answer and you will never look at your life in the same way.

And you will certainly never look back.

Caroline Barth,
Head of Global HR, Novartis Pharmaceuticals

ACKNOWLEDGEMENTS

Thank you universe for the best, wildest, most challenging and incredible ride of my life. The writing of this book and launch of TarinaW.com, while still running LifeWorks and my home, has truly tested my abilities and skills. Thank you for stretching me professionally and mentally, and for the abundance of choices we are provided with daily. Thank you for presenting us with all kinds of options to seize, obstacles to overcome, and for the endless possibilities to live life as beautifully as we make it to be.

A most deep and sincere thank you to my readers, clients, students, and mentors. You have all provided me with the wisdom and connection that inspires what I aim to achieve every day. Your humanity, hope, honesty, and goodness is exactly what this world needs, and by pursuing your own deliberate lives, you will each begin a ripple effect that will change our communities and our world.

To my editor, Anna: how was there even a world before you were in my life? How did I not know that such skill, talent, and beauty existed in such a perfect combination? You came into my life and swept me away in head and heart. You are a brilliant editor, writer, and artist. You have the long-term strategic vision and the short-term savvy to make it all happen. You are a creator and an adviser, you are relentless and truly Annadorable. I love you like my family and can't wait to meet your babies one day and hug them tight. No words could ever articulate my gratitude for how you brought this book and my brand to life. You have treated it all as your own and given me permission to be myself (under your considerate eye!) every day. I have loved teaching and learning from each other and am deeply humbled by your extraordinary remarkableness as a colleague, friend, and human being. You have spun this book with pure gold.

To my husband, Robert, who has taken our 22-year marriage to a new level through our work on this book and creating this new branch of my business together: not only have you made every single meal and smoothie I have enjoyed every single day through the launch of this all – most importantly, you have allowed me, with such grace, to share the most intimate, difficult parts of our lives with others in the hopes it will make a difference to them. I truly do not believe I could have dreamt up a better husband and father on this planet. You are my biggest supporter in life and the best partner I could ask for. I admire you in countless and overwhelming ways. Your endless love and support allow me to do what I do every day. One thing I know for sure: all of this – this wild, amazing journey – was only possible with you by my side.

To my dad, who didn't live to see this second book but who I know would have been tremendously proud: like I said in your eulogy, "It's time to put pen to paper and let music back into my heart." I have dad. Our story may not have been an easy one, but I know that, as a talented writer yourself, you would have supported me sharing it with others in this way.

To my mama bear bird of mine: thank you for making me turn towards deliberateness and feel like your most special girl, always and forever. From you, I have learned true love and what it means to be both a daughter and a mom. And from you and dad, in the years you were so very in love, for showing me what true intimacy in a partnership is. A coupling so close that you each shouted, "Changing levels!" when going up or down the stairs so that you'd always know where to find each other. With your example, Robert and I are so close and connected in this same way. With all the things I do in my home and in our family – nothing compares to your capacity for love, which I was lucky enough to call mine every moment of every day, which has made my life filled to the brim with sunshine and stars.

To my Board of Directors, all carefully chosen and wholeheartedly cherished: thank you. First – Caroline, my true teacher of Beauty, who in NYC's Central Park found the title with me. My amazing Aunt Terri (and Uncle Bruce!) who spent countless hours on text with me at the drop of a dime on any workday to get the perfect title and book cover that was ME, and for teaching me Suitcases and Umbrellas. My brother Steve and sister-in-law Sandy, who taught me the ropes in so many ways through discussions and inspiration. Thank you for your constant, consistent love and support for me and my family in countless aspects of our lives. Stephanie, for being my go-to loving rock for amazing advice and career discussions that have carved my path. Carroll, my true love since Grade 4, for your undying love, generosity and encouragement, and for articulating love in action as a phrase you used long ago to describe me. Cheryl and Colleen, for being the kind of moms and friends that give this book a lot of content when it comes to loving and showing it. Christian Marcolli, my teacher of performance and potential, for exposing me to the success of our first co-authored book, *More Life, Please!* and for telling me long ago to reach for the high fruits on the trees and for believing that I could do it. Robert Shereck, my teacher of transformation, thank you for everything good in my life and for making me come complete with others' capabilities. And for saving my precious marriage – for real.

My BFF, Leah sister savvy, who is my purest example of Deliberateness in every way and who has allowed me to be carried on your brilliant coattails in so many ways in family life, travel, financial decisions, and overall brilliance and savvy directions. You are the smartest and most Deliberate person I know. Thank you for starting me on this path of Deliberateness by your sheer example and for supporting me so incredibly along the way. Every pep text is the highlight of everyday, week, month, and year. You make my life so beautiful in ways I never would have known without you.

To Vanessa, my BFF soul-keeper, to whom I owe much of my life, truly. You challenge me each and every day to be more of the best version of myself through your incredible devotion and support and pure unconditional love of me. Being your person is like falling into the arms of the most wonderful, kind, welcoming love known to human kind, and I cannot believe each and every day that I get to call you mine. You taught me how to fully love all the people I already adored and to live that love without judgement or fear. You taught me how to live again and forgive and have brought a beauty and grace into my life that I would never have experienced or known without you. You are an amazing example of the type of person and parent we should all aspire to be.

To all my family and friends who helped me with the title and book cover and who were always available for quick and precious feedback.

To all the amazing people and leaders I have coached, who let me into their lives with such full authenticity. I learned everything in this book from the precious sharing of your hearts, souls and minds. And to all the great corporate success examples I have in my life through the thousands I have coached, trained, learned and collaborated with throughout my career. To name a few examples of amazing collaborations: Bristol-Myers Squibb, Novartis, Peak Performance2, The Usheroff Institute, Marcolli Executive Excellence, NGen, BAT, Paladin, Sanofi, Dama, and the list goes on and on. I am so grateful for your confidence and trust in me.

To all the wonderful books I have learned from that have been my guiding compasses. By reading a minimum of 60 non-fiction books each and every year, my mind is filled with the brilliance of so many talented leaders, authors, and speakers who have been my North Stars.

To Peggy McColl, the brilliant businesswoman and millionaire author-maker who shared her home and her remarkable brain with me to get me started on my way, strategically. To Hasmark Publishing who were true business partners in bringing my book to life. To my amazing web designer, Corinna, for the best listening of a lifetime, and to my dedicated team of videographers and producers for their work on TarinaW.com.

Most of all, thank you to my three children. Every single day, I have wanted and aspired to do more and be more, be balanced and deliberate, for you and our family.

I promised myself I would never access this book in myself until I was fully convinced you were all happy, resilient, confidant, and successful in all the ways that make you happy in your lives, and I am so pleased to say that time has come. I am sure now that I contributed to something very, very right (along with yourselves and daddy). You have given me content for this book every single day, and it feels so good to share it all with the world.

To Nicholas (20), who is my heartbeat and who is my very best business buddy and passionate partner of all that is life. I am astounded by the confidence, charisma, and raw talent you possess that knocks me off my feet every time you enter a room. You are an incredible son, brother, and human being, and you impress me so much with your devotion, dedication, passion and intelligence. You saying, "I love you, mom" so many times a day since you were born and cuddling and co-existing with us is my greatest pride ever.

To Tristan (18), my true inspiration – someone whom I admire in terms of drive, leadership, determination and pure goodness, and combining it all so powerfully and beautifully into the perfect package of one incredible human being and son. From the moment you were born, I knew you were special and there is not a day that goes by that I am truly not in awe that I was part of growing you from a seed and seeing you flourish and bloom into the extraordinary human being you are today. I learn from you and your example every single day.

Last but not least, my beautiful daughter Emma (16), who has ultimately taught me that it is possible to be the parent I always knew I could be deep inside myself. You have taught me the importance of adapting and connecting to the ones we love most and the power and impact of that kind of love. Of everyone I know in the world, I admire your mental and physical resilience the most. You are by far the strongest teenager I have ever come across and you manage your complex life and energy in a way that is truly admirable and inspirational. To watch you alone onstage dancing in front of hundreds of people and winning over and over again has been the biggest gift for all of us and a transcendent experience of sheer beauty and grace. Through you, I have been able to truly repair with gold all the cracks of my parenting and heart. You are my heart's finale of true devotion, adaptability and love. You remind me daily to never, ever give up on the buckets and bins that are most important to you and of the precious gift of laser-focus when it really counts.

With deep appreciation and gratitude to our human ability to say no to many things, yes to lots of others, and the choice to make the moments of our lives valuable and remarkable in a way that matters to us most.

Play by your own rules and love every minute of this beautiful, terrifying, messy, awesome one life you have the gift of living.

Praise for **Working with Tarina W.**

"*Before working with Tarina, we didn't have the focus on what we wanted to accomplish. When Tarina entered our life at Sanofi, she provided us with clarity and excitement about our goals and made sure our needs were addressed before, during and after the training workshops. Her contagious energy and masterful coaching skills were immediately transposed to the team and became a sense of inspiration for all. Her flexibility, adaptability and strategic mind brought the whole team to a new level of engagement and commitment. Tarina treated our work together as a journey, not solely a destination – she focuses on what matters most, sustainable high performance and leadership. She has a human approach and her model is simple and remarkably effective. I highly recommend working with her!*"

– Isabelle Deslauriers,
Head of Sales and Operation at Sanofi Canada

"*Empathetic. Remarkable. Audacious. These are just a few words that come to mind when thinking about Tarina. Working with her has given me the confidence to shift the way I position myself in a professional setting. She has helped me understand my value and feel deserving of the successes that have come my way as a result. Her expertise and guidance has definitely allowed me to be best version of myself!*"

– Aristea Danopoulos,
Salesforce Effectiveness Lead at Bristol-Myers Squibb Canada

"*In working with Tarina, she was able to tap into a potential I always felt I had but had trouble bringing to the surface. She allowed me to gain perspective and clarity on my abilities and who I am fundamentally so that I was able to bring my performance and quality of life to the next level. I am now a more confident person and much better leader in all aspects of my life because of her and her profound approach.*"

– Andrew Beaulieu,
Manager, Service Division at Dama Construction

"Having known and worked collaboratively with Tarina in the financial sector for more than two decades provides me with great perspective to underscore her abilities as a veritable leader in promoting work-life integration. Her ability to synthesize complex information and apply it to the fundamentals of daily life and business is truly remarkable. Her deliberate, no-nonsense approach applied to her own career has resulted in business revenues that have tripled in one year. Use Tarina's brilliance to achieve the life and financial success you have always known is within your grasp! She has every skill you need to show you how to live a more abundant life in every sense of the word and will be your guide every step of the way as she has done with countless professionals."

– Jeremy Hampson,
Senior Wealth Advisor at Assante Wealth Management

"As a senior executive running a global organization, I am confident in saying that Tarina has regularly addressed my observations and concerns. She has provided tangible objectives for me and my business. Her ability to provide clarity has not only driven practical and actionable strategies for my business, but has also helped me discover self-confidence and inner peace. Ultimately, her approach to my world has driven success in my career, ensuring a balanced approach to my family life, relationships with friends, and personal objectives. Listen to her."

– Ian Locke,
Vice President at BJG Electronics

"I have had the privilege of co-facilitating with Tarina over many years, and I am always inspired by her compassion, charisma and connection with everyone that crosses her path. She is a master facilitator who has the ability to guide and teach on many diverse subjects with ease and skill. As a powerful thought leader, coupled with her intuitiveness and practical wisdom, Tarina positions her clients for success both personally and professionally. Anyone who has the privilege of working with Tarina will acquire deeper insights into living life to the fullest."

– Roz Usheroff,
President of The Usheroff Institute

"*Initially, the thought of working with a professional coach was met with slight resistance on my part. As a quasi-introvert, discussing matters in life and business openly aren't easily accessible from me. My mindset quickly changed as soon as our work together began. Tarina is true professional with a coaching technique that 'got me,' which allowed me to break out to deliver my A-game in my demanding role. She exceeded my expectations and I can confidently say that she has been one of the few professionals I've felt comfortable opening up to, without reservation. Working with her will make a massive difference in your life!*"

– Andre Denischuck,
Regional Sales Director of Central Canada
at Imperial Tobacco Company Limited

"*Tarina is one of our finest DYNAMIX and Team Performance consultants, coaches, and facilitators. She completely walks the talk, is the expert of balancing work and home life and helps bring this magic into the lives of her clients so profoundly. Tarina asks great questions that make you really think and always challenges others to become their best. If you want to take more control of your life and your future, without a doubt read her book and take her programs.*"

– Paul Fergus,
President of Peak Performance2

"*Tarina lives her values boldly and with pride, in her communication, in her work with leaders and with her family. I have seen Tarina do this for others, displaying the utmost respect for their uniqueness, always curious to learn about what makes them tick and what is important to them, all with the underlying purpose of helping them live a remarkable life – not in a text book kind of way, but in a keeping-it-real approach. I thoroughly enjoy working side by side with Tarina and love the learning that comes from it. She is truly the master of living a remarkable life!*"

– Candace Seniw,
Senior Managing Director of Strategic Avenue Consulting

"*Something special happens when people work with Tarina: mountains are climbed, relationships are strengthened, and a sense of ease and possibility becomes the new norm. With compassion, relentlessness, and unmatched vision, Tarina is the exact kind of person you want on your team.*"

– Anna Rosenfield,
Learning Consultant and Editor

"*If you have any areas in your life that you feel aren't optimal, it's a complete no-brainer to pick Tarina's brain and books. We have applied several of her masterful ideas and strategies to our own life challenges and have enjoyed incredible success. This book will enable you to think differently in a proactive and strategic way, both professionally and personally. This is an absolute must read – Tarina is sure to get you into action!*"

– Michael Bury,
Associate Ombudsman, McGill University Health Centres

"*Tarina tells it like it is and knows exactly what you need to hear to take action in your life and live deliberately. She is an incredible coach who has the ability to listen and guide you through the steps it takes to lead a meaningful deliberate life. She has been an invaluable force in my life for many years and has guided and taught me how to implement systems and strategies and new ways of thinking that are truly life changing for me and my family. Her book is a must read for anyone wanting to reach their full potential and live life to the fullest!*"

– Leah Davidson,
Speech Language Pathologist and
Owner/Luxury Travel Advisor of Leah Davidson Travel

"*Tarina provided me with extremely valuable insight and coaching and offered out of the box ways of thinking when I was making a major career change to follow my passion. With Tarina's help I was able to make the right decision for my life and my happiness and have never looked back since!*"

– Cheryl Adams,
Lodging Consultant for Seniors

"*Tarina has practiced a life of dedication to her family and career, balancing both with a sense of purpose and devotion. Her extensive interest in and love of researching and implementing practices to improve relationships is a wonderful example. She has a genuine passion for dealing with the daily struggles and conflicts of family life. No matter how real the issue, Tarina addresses it in an honest and human way. I am grateful to have her on the parent journey with me!*"

**– Colleen Murphy,
Mom of 4**

"*Tarina has the unique ability to pull out your truest feelings and your deepest values, then transform them into creative and effective action to get what you most want in life. She has found that magic triangle of profound deliberateness!*"

**– Carroll Wilson,
Social Worker and Psychotherapist**

"*Tarina is a master facilitator and speaker and possesses the rare quality of being able to easily connect with her audience in an authentic way. She is highly relatable, wickedly engaging and passionate about what she does, which comes through in her dynamic delivery style that keeps audiences of all sizes interested and eager to learn more.*"

**– Giselle Kovary,
President of n-gen People Performance Inc.**

"*I have had the pleasure of working with Tarina in two different companies where I was a participant to her leadership trainings. She is a master facilitator who stands out from others as she is highly skilled and knowledgeable, has contagious and genuine energy and continually challenges the group to bring us to a whole new level. As a leader, her training and guidance have helped me become a better coach within my teams and have transformed my interactions both with my employees as well as those in my personal life. I am convinced the same will happen for you when you work with Tarina. Make it happen!*"

**– Melanie Paquet,
Area Business Manager at Sanofi Pharmaceuticals Canada**

DO YOU WANT TO TAKE YOUR DELIBERATE LIFE TO THE NEXT LEVEL?

YOUR JOURNEY DOESN'T HAVE TO END HERE.

For most of us, life is hectic.

For all of us, life is precious.

That's why for over 17 years, Tarina W. has been helping thousands of people like you tackle the distractions in their lives and get them on track to a life of more purpose and joy, one shaped by their highest values, priorities, and dreams.

You can feel you're finally accessing your potential in
your relationships, career, and bank account.

You can find peace and confidence in your decisions.

You can have a life that reflects your
dreams and not your fears.

Go to **www.TarinaW.com** to discover Tarina's online workshops, 1-1 mentoring and group mastermind that will empower you with the clarity and confidence you need to bridge the gap between where you are and where you want to be. In this age of distraction Tarina will guide you towards deliberateness so that you have more time and energy for the things that matter most to you.

This is your one life as you – it deserves your full attention.

*Follow Tarina on social media for
your weekly tips, tricks, and stories at
@tarinawofficial*

BIBLIOGRAPHY

Bryan, William J. "William Jennings Bryan Quotes." Goodreads.com. https://www.goodreads.com/author/quotes/310550.William_Jennings_Bryan (accessed June 11th, 2018)

Durant, Will. "Will Durant Quotes." Brainyquote.com. https://www.brainyquote.com/quotes/will_durant_145967 (accessed May 30th, 2018).

Fleming, Victor, dir. *The Wizard of Oz*. 1939; Culver City, CA: Metro-Goldwyn-Mayer, 2005, DVD.

Forleo, Marie. "Everything is Figureoutable: My Oprah Supersoul Session." MarieForleo.com. https://www.marieforleo.com/2016/05/everything-is-figureoutable/ (accessed June 4th, 2018).

Gilbert, Elizabeth. 2015. *Big Magic: Creative Living Beyond Fear*. New York: Penguin Books.

Godin, Seth. 2009. *Purple Cow: Transform Your Business by Being Remarkable*. New York: Portfolio.

Huffington, Arianna. 2014. *Thrive: The Third Metric to Redefining Success and Creating a Life of Well-Being, Wisdom, and Wonder*. New York: Harmony Books.

James, William. "William James Quotes." Brainyquote.com. https://www.brainyquote.com/quotes/william_james_105643 (accessed May 31st, 2018).

"Kintsukuroi – More Beautiful for Having Been Broken." Camiimac.com. http://www.camiimac.com/good-juju-today-blog/kintsukuroi-more-beautiful-for-having-been-broken. (accessed June 15, 2018).

"Locus of Control." Changingminds.org. http://changingminds.org/explanations/preferences/locus_control.htm (accessed May 2nd, 2018).

Martino, Joe. "Someone Asked the Dalai Lama What Surprises Him Most, His Response was Mind Altering." Collective-evolution.com. https://www.collective-evolution.com/2014/05/25/someone-asked-the-dalai-lama-what-surprises-him-most-his-response-was-mind-altering/ (accessed May 9th, 2018).

Perel, Esther. "About Me". Estherperel.com. https://www.estherperel.com/my-story (accessed May 31st, 2018).

Popova, Maria. "How We Spend Our Days Is How We Spend Our Lives: Annie Dillard on Choosing Presence Over Productivity." Brainpickings.org. https://www.brainpickings.org/2013/06/07/annie-dillard-the-writing-life-1/ (accessed May 9th, 2018).

Vanderkam, Laura. 2011. *168 Hours: You Have More Time Than You Think*. New York: Penguin Press

Verner, Amy. "L'Oreal's 'Because I'm Worth It' Slogan Marks a Milestone." Theglobeandmail.com. https://www.theglobeandmail.com/life/fashion-and-beauty/beauty/loreals-because-im-worth-it-slogan-marks-a-milestone/article554604/ (accessed May 11th, 2018).

ABOUT THE AUTHOR

Tarina W. is an #1 international bestselling author, global learning strategist, international corporate speaker, and executive performance coach committed to helping people live a life of presence and purpose that matters to them.

She is the president of *Tarina W.* and *Life Works Solutions*, training thousands and coaching hundreds around the globe in some of today's most compelling personal development and sustainable high performance strategies. She has worked with everyone from CEOs in top Fortune 500 companies to stay-at-home parents, earning the reputation for being a gold standard expert in strategic, deliberate action, personal and professional high performance, and bringing your unique value to visibility.

She lives in Montreal, Canada with her husband and three children, but her heart belongs with them all at her lakeside cottage in the Laurentian Mountains.

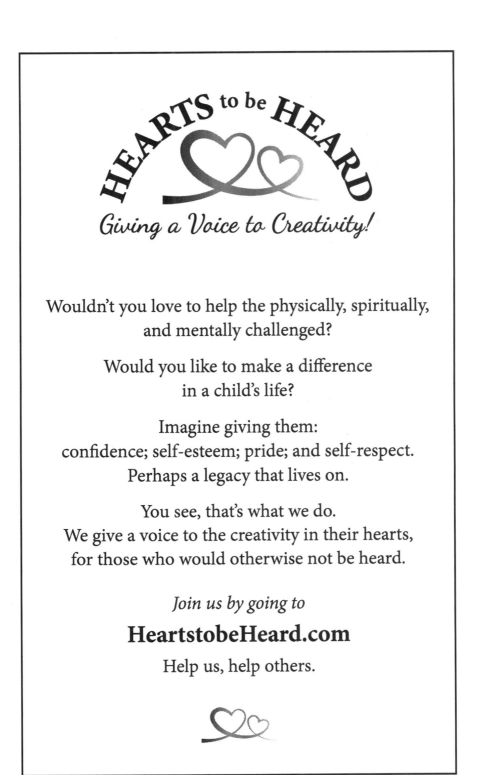

Hearts to be **HEARD**

Giving a Voice to Creativity!

Wouldn't you love to help the physically, spiritually,
and mentally challenged?

Would you like to make a difference
in a child's life?

Imagine giving them:
confidence; self-esteem; pride; and self-respect.
Perhaps a legacy that lives on.

You see, that's what we do.
We give a voice to the creativity in their hearts,
for those who would otherwise not be heard.

Join us by going to

HeartstobeHeard.com

Help us, help others.

Made in the USA
Lexington, KY
24 January 2019